DAVID THAUBERGER
PAINTINGS 1978-1988

Peter White

with an essay by
Nancy Tousley

Organized and circulated by
Mackenzie Art Gallery with
support from The Canada Council

Sponsored by
TransCanada PipeLines
through its Arts Development Program

David Thauberger: Paintings 1978—1988

ISBN 0-920922-52-X

©The contributors and the
Norman Mackenzie Art Gallery 1988

Publisher: Norman Mackenzie Art Gallery
          University of Regina
          Regina, Saskatchewan
          Canada S4S 0A2

Design: Brian Wood Design Studio, Regina

Printing: Houghton Boston,
Saskatoon, Saskatchewan, Canada

Photography: All photography is by Don Hall,
AV Services, University of Regina, except figures
7 and 8, which are courtesy Glenbow Museum,
Calgary, and fig. 11, which is by Terry
Cuddington.

The exhibition has been organized by the
Norman Mackenzie Art Gallery with support
from The Canada Council.

Sponsored by

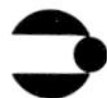

TransCanada PipeLines
Through its Arts Development Program

Exhibition Schedule

Mackenzie Art Gallery
University of Regina
Regina, Saskatchewan
7 October — 4 December 1988

Memorial University Art Gallery
St. John's, Newfoundland
12 January — 19 February 1989

The Koffler Gallery
The Koffler Centre of the Arts
Toronto, Ontario
6 March — 13 April 1989

Art Gallery of Windsor
Windsor, Ontario
13 May — 18 June 1989

Mendel Art Gallery
Saskatoon, Saskatchewan
6 July — 27 August 1989

Winnipeg Art Gallery
Winnipeg, Manitoba
23 September — 29 October 1989

The Nickle Arts Museum
The University of Calgary
Calgary, Alberta
1 December 1989 — 7 January 1990

Cover: *Doll's House* 1988 (cat. 39)

CONTENTS

PREFACE

TransCanada PipeLines, through its Arts Development Program, is proud to sponsor the first comprehensive survey exhibition of David Thauberger's paintings. With this national touring exhibition, the accomplishments of Mr. Thauberger will be presented to a great many Canadians for the first time. The project is a fine example of the artistic endeavours being supported by TransCanada's Arts Development Program — a three-year effort aimed at supporting artists and developing new audiences in Canada.

We would like to thank Peter White, curator of the exhibition, and Andrew Oko, director of the Mackenzie Art Gallery, for their commitment to the show's success. We also extend our appreciation to David Thauberger for the remarkable body of work he has made available for presentation.

G. J. Maier
President and Chief Executive Officer
TransCanada PipeLines

FOREWORD

The exhibition and collection of works by Canadian artists is a major mandate of the Mackenzie Art Gallery. David Thauberger is a major artist of national stature. The gallery is delighted, then, to present this first comprehensive survey exhibition of the artist's paintings for national tour.

Since 1978, David Thauberger's concerns in his paintings have centered on the exploration of cultural themes emanating from his own life in Saskatchewan. The resulting body of work is a potent statement of the role of culture in shaping our understanding of reality. On behalf of the gallery, I would like to thank the artist most sincerely for sharing this vision by his commitment to the project.

It has been a pleasure working with Peter White, Curator/Director of the Dunlop Art Gallery in Regina and guest curator for this exhibition. His active involvement with contemporary Canadian art and artists, and his appreciation of David Thauberger's concerns, made him the natural choice to curate the exhibition. I would also like to express our appreciation to art critic Nancy Tousley of Calgary for contributing her essay on the artist's work. Together, Peter White and Nancy Tousley have provided in this publication a sensitive and thorough review of the artist's work.

A nationally touring exhibition involves the loan of work for well over a year. The lenders have been most generous. We are deeply grateful.

The photography for this publication by Don Hall, AV Services, University of Regina, must be acknowledged. Sally Hennessy and Janet Conover of Arts and Communications Counselors of Toronto have been supportive from the outset. I would also like to thank the gallery's staff for their assistance with the many phases of the project.

Finally, on behalf of the Norman Mackenzie Art Gallery, I would like to thank The Canada Council for their support, and gratefully acknowledge the sponsorship of the exhibition by TransCanada PipeLines through its Arts Development Program.

Andrew Oko
Director

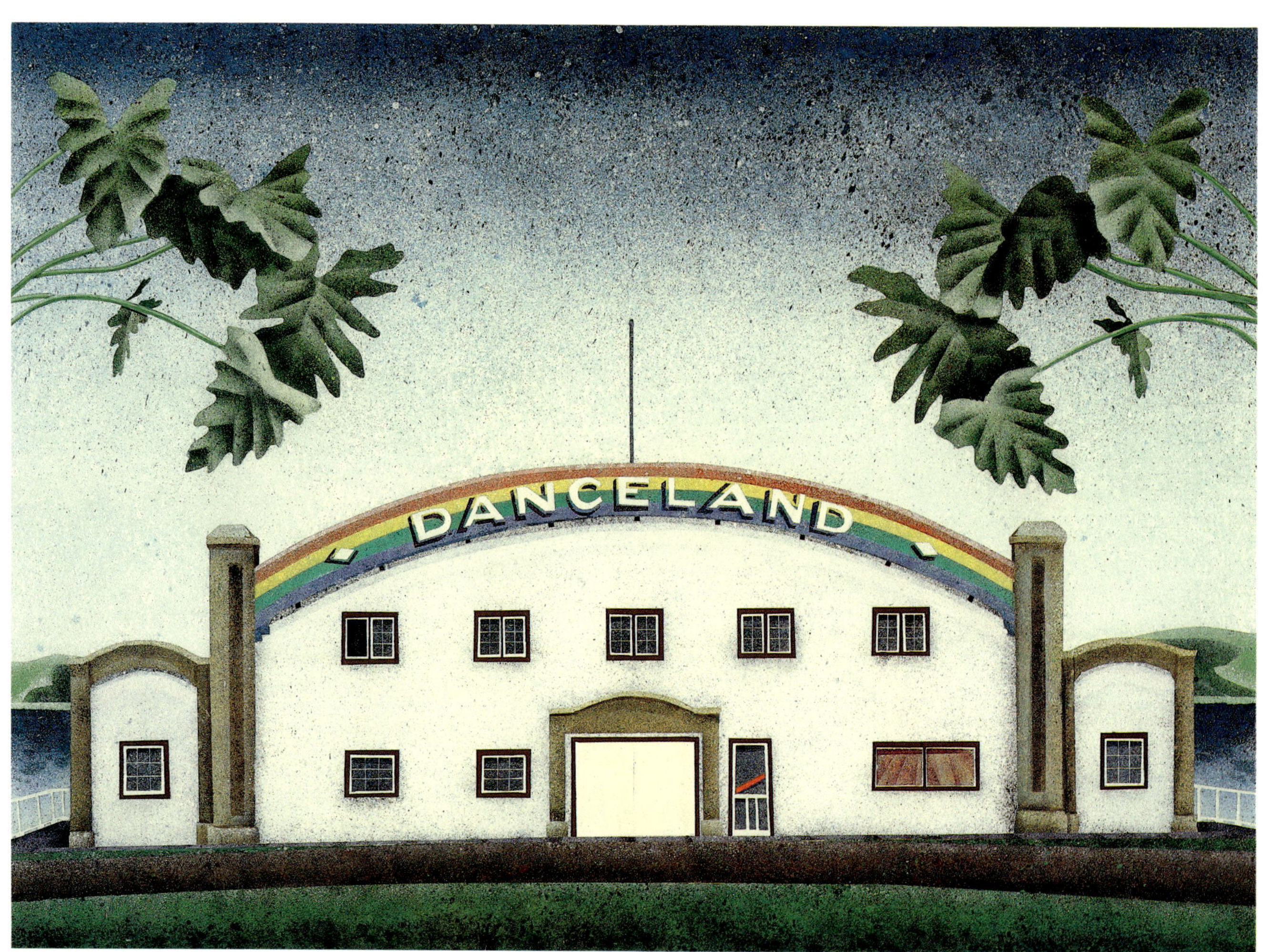

Plate 1 *Rainbow Danceland* 1979 (cat. 6)

PUTTING THINGS IN PLACE:
DAVID THAUBERGER'S VERNACULAR STYLE

Nancy Tousley

I cannot separate the place where I work
from the place where I live. One can
really inhabit one's place. Wherever
that may be.

Michel Nedjar
I Am Tied to the Threads of the World[1]

Consider the matter of David Thauberger's regionalism. To Thauberger's way of thinking, all art is regional in that it arises from a particular culture, at a particular time, in a particular part of the world. Certainly, the world has become too small and yet remains too large for the concerns of his work to be encompassed by a regionalism defined as it has been in the past by the literal description of a place or the imprint made by geography on the inhabitants of the land. Strong bodies of work in the visual arts and literature redefine foregoing conditions and Thauberger's work has done this. The central position in his iconography *is* occupied by place. But when we choose the term regionalism to circumscribe it, Thauberger's conception of place immediately announces its difference — through the artist's self-awareness, the double perspective of his close observations and the distinctive character of his assertive stylistic voice.

Thauberger's awareness is not just regional; it is cosmopolitan and regional at the same time. He focuses not on geography, but the sensibility of a place and the attitudes that connect it to a larger world. His unique painter's voice speaks in a visual patois that combines the accents and inflections of vernacular and popular culture with the syntax of modernism. Indeed, regionalism is inscribed in the history of his place. But what appears in his work to be regional might better be ascribed to Thauberger's interest in the ''local,'' in his locale, the place into which he was born and has chosen to live and work.[2]

Yet, it's probably significant that Thauberger has chosen not to name his place in the manner of the fiction writer. We recognize the locale as Regina, but Thauberger extends the city limits to include the outlying districts and small towns like Holdfast, where he was born in 1948, or Manitou Beach or Penzance. Although his place is urban, it has rural and small town roots that the artist also makes visible; these roots nourish its history and establish the network that defines its perimeter in southern Saskatchewan. It's a place that has accommodated anachronism, change and the movement of people off the land into cities and towns. Thauberger's choice has been to construct a cluster of locales whose boundary is marked only by the limits of his own attentive gaze. Each locale remains visually distinct as a fixed point in time and space, but through the network of inter-relationships within the body of his work, Thauberger maintains a continuity between the present and the past.

The terms locale and region are always contingent on a frame of reference — geography, economics, politics, customs and folkways, time periods and even one's personal understanding of

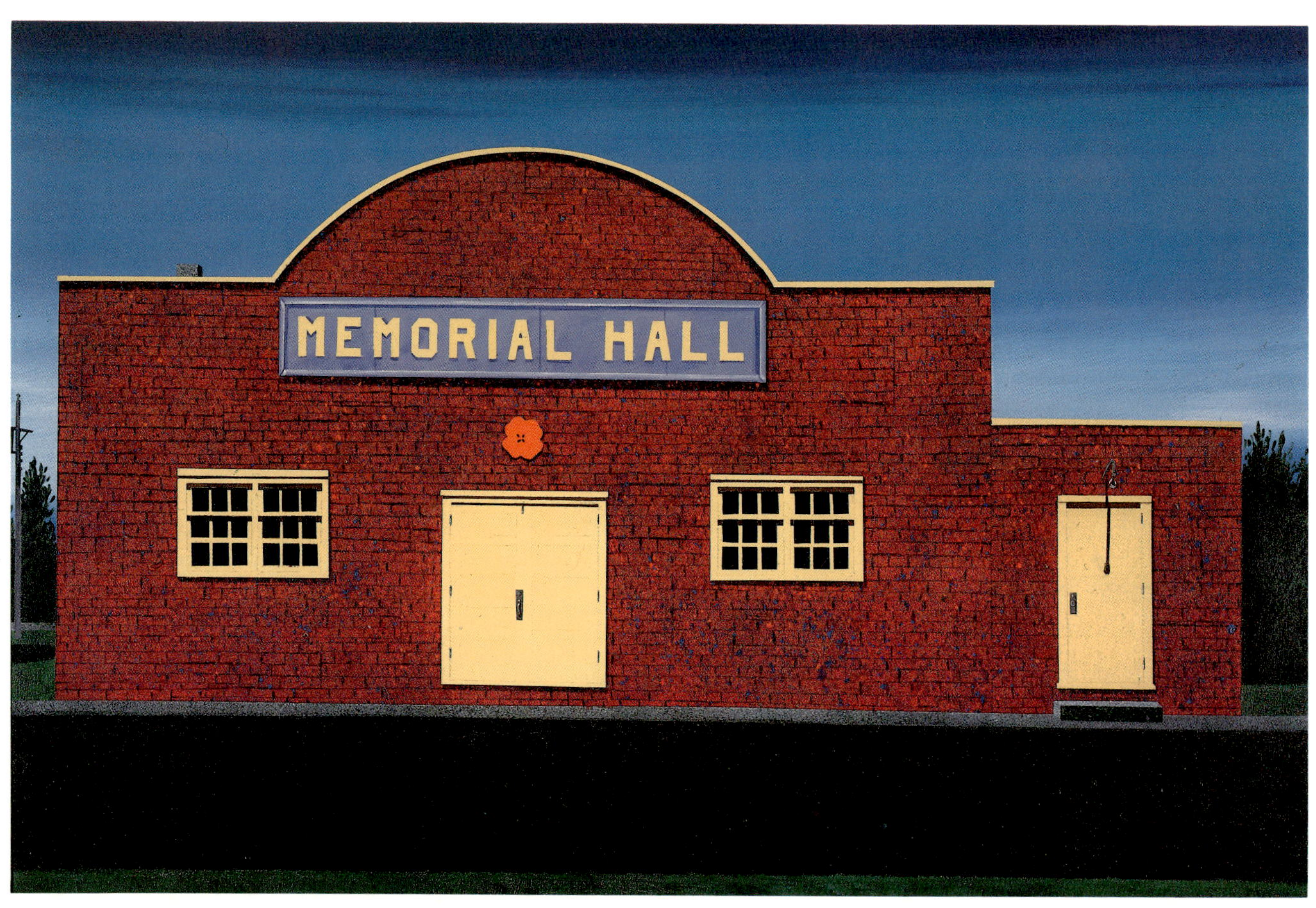

Plate 2 *Dance Hall* 1980 (cat. 10)

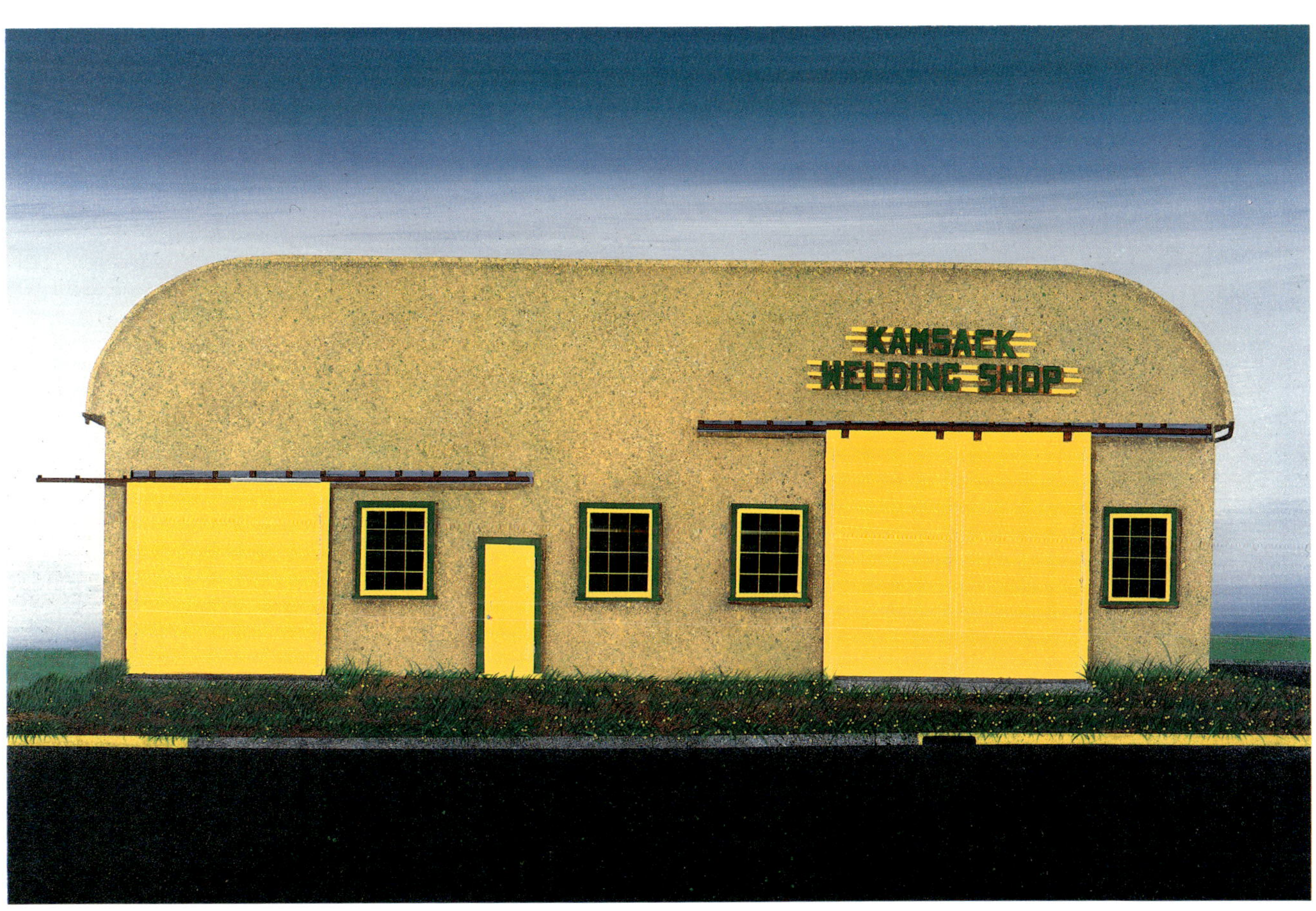

Plate 3 *Bread and Butter* 1980 (cat. 9)

what constitutes a place. The place Thauberger defines exists as a moment of delicate equilibrium between the static world of his childhood and the changing world he knows as an adult. The recent and the distant pasts are, for him, necessary reference points within a modern world in constant flux. As Flannery O'Connor told a group of fellow Georgia writers in the early 1960s: "In the past, the things that have seemed to many to make us ourselves have been very obvious things, but now no amount of nostalgia can make us believe they will characterize us much longer."[3]

Thauberger views his place with a double vision. He fixes locale in all of its particulars and locates it in the larger framework of contemporary culture. It's as though two somewhat different representations of the same place were being thrown into relief by a stereoscope. Where, on the one hand, Thauberger shares the regionalist's attachment to the particular, the familiar detail that calls to mind the entire ethos of a time and place, on the other, he uses these particulars to construct a locale that exists simultaneously as the representation of an actual place and as a place in the mind. He represents place not as it is, but as he sees and experiences it through a sensibility formed by his childhood memories, his knowledge of art, his love of popular culture and his regard for the attitudes, gestures and values of the local community itself.

Place and community are inseparable in Thauberger's work. It is the community that defines the place, builds its structures and provides its varying textures. Thauberger recovers and examines its overlooked material culture, the things that show how the community has shaped and altered itself, what it values, takes pleasure in, dreams of, and remembers. In the past, prairie regionalism kept an eye on the far horizon, and looked self-consciously to the impact of the land on the psyche as the determinant factor of regional identity. Thauberger has exchanged the prairie landscape vista for the close-up view, raising the magnification power of his eye and focusing it on the built and lived-in environment. This is a settled place, a layered space within which the present and the past, the individual idiosyncrasy and the communal expression, the local culture and the influence of mass communications all intermingle.

Thauberger's iconography is pervaded by images of architecture, signs of habitation and social congress: farm house, barn, grain elevator, dance hall, Masonic temple, Legion hall, church, small business, glass tower, inner-city bungalow, suburban villa, and, even, mileposts of modernity — the Crystal Palace (pl. 13), built in London to house the Great International Exhibition of 1851,[4] and the 1939/40 New York World's Fair (pls. 25-28) — which captured imaginations worldwide. These images catalogue the social reality, the values and fantasies of a place in a multi-layered portrayal. Collectively, they cannot be taken simply as a representative sampling of local colour or local architectural styles because, individually, they in turn are layered. Plucked from actuality, isolated and transformed, each found image exists simultaneously as fact and symbol.

Thauberger selects these architectural images with the eye of an artist, an iconographer, an archaeologist, a cultural historian and a connoisseur of the off-beat. The farm house, a generic symbol of agrarian life, is also his grandfather's house, memorialized in *Grandfather's Painting,* 1978 (pl. 11). The plain prairie dance hall, an historical artifact of the 1920s, remains a palace of romance and dreams seen through a glamorizing scrim of nostalgia in *Rainbow Danceland,* 1979 (pl. 1). An eccentric bit of vernacular building, the yellow, loaf-shaped Kamsack Welding Shop in *Bread and Butter,* 1980 (pl. 3), becomes an artifact of popular culture and a symbol of the dignity and value

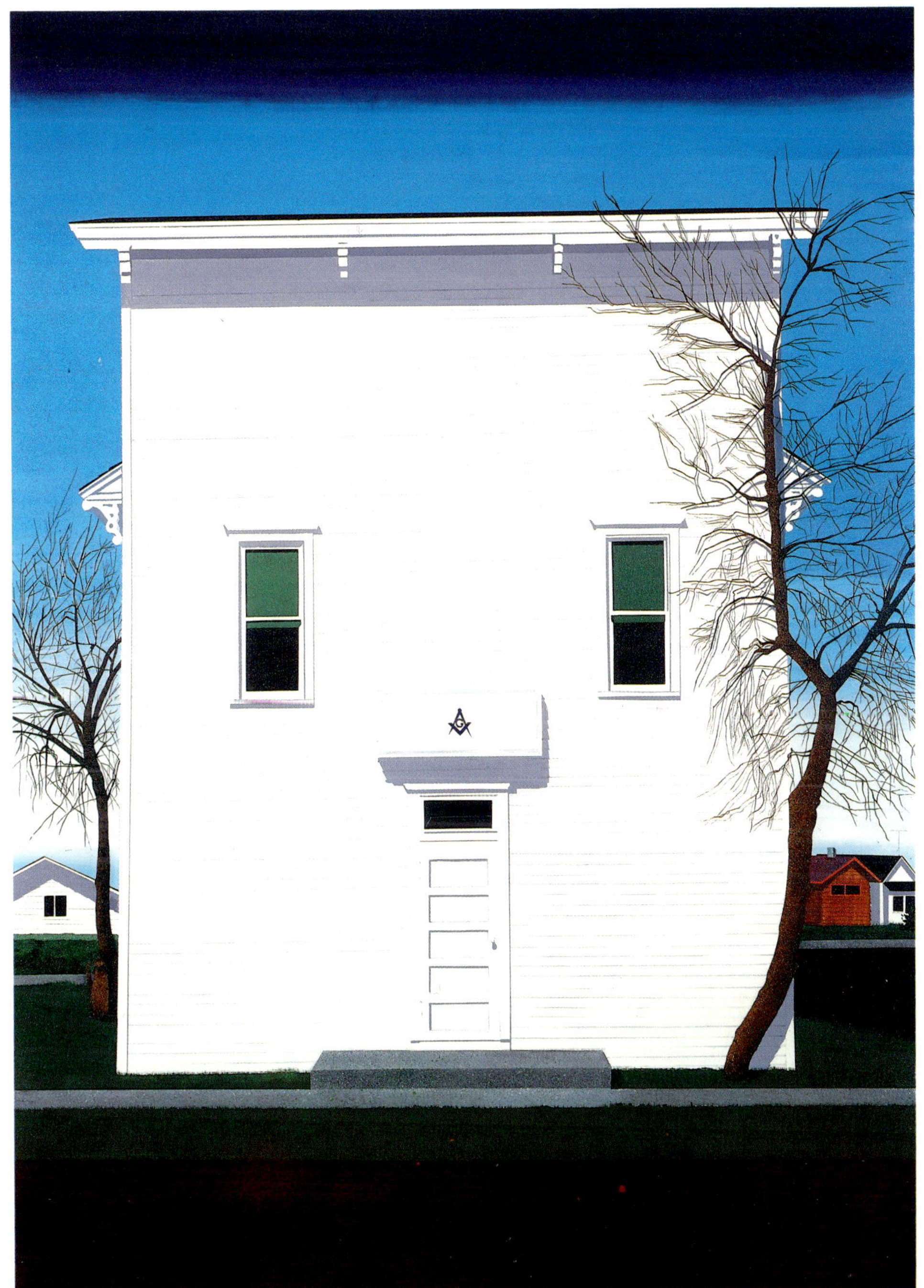

Plate 4 *White Hall* 1981 (cat. 16)

of work. The halcyon villa in *Pride of Ownership* (pl. 34) and the splendid architectural period piece in *50s Split* (fig. 14), both 1987, locate middle-class aspirations for the good life in suburbia and place them in the context of consumerism and suburban development.

Representations of taste and sensibility enter Thauberger's work through architectural styles, the decoration and ornamentation of facades, the landscaping and planting of lawns. Churches, lodges and the Women's Institute shown in *Kachina,* 1981 (pl. 6), embody the community's spiritual and fraternal life. Postcard inspired landscapes of scenic wonders and other marvels such as Easter Island, seen in *Driving Rain,* 1984 (pl. 24), far away *Machu Picchu,* 1984 (pl. 7), the *Observation Point,* 1983 (pl. 22) at Niagara Falls, the *Big Geyser,* 1983 (pl. 8) at Yellowstone National Park, the *Crystal Palace,* 1979, or the humble traveller's rest in *Motel — 24 Channels,* 1985 (fig. 12), point to the community's taste for the exotic and its own leisure travel as well as to its armchair tourist's fascination with other places of the mind. For the places most people in the hinterlands never get to can be seen on television or visited via postcards and the photographs in calendars and magazines. Early in his painting career, when Thauberger chose the *Crystal Palace* to represent communal imagination and sensibility, his selection of site was particularly apt. Marshall Berman has pointed out that, ''where the process of modernization has not yet come into its own, modernism, where it develops, takes on a fantastic character, because it is forced to nourish itself not on social reality but on fantasies, mirages, dreams.''[5]

The people themselves never appear in these paintings. Thauberger represents the objects of their making, the objects of their desires and the objects of their affections — the things that bind them together as a social unit within a larger society. The one peopled work in this chronicle of place represents a team photograph. Painted in 1980 from a postcard, *Green and White Painting (Dobberville)* (pl. 5) shows rows of uniformed football players in unmatching socks lined up on outdoor bleachers. Although their image might represent any local college or high school team and, by inference, team spirit, the reference is specific. These are the Saskatchewan Roughriders of Thauberger's boyhood in the early 1950s, a motley team led by star quarterback Glen Dobbs. Team spirit is very much the point, but team spirit magnified into fervour. Dobbs and the Roughriders became folk heroes and mail addressed to Dobberville reached Regina. The team's efforts put Saskatchewan on the map. Whether or not the Roughriders won every game hardly seemed to matter; they won peoples' hearts and fired their collective imagination. As folk heroes, the Roughriders hold a special place in Thauberger's iconography. If he were to insert other ordinary individuals into his place, they would of necessity become characters. That would destroy the clarity and symmetry of his double vision. The main character, the determinant of identity played out in Thauberger's locale, is culture.

Thauberger approaches the culture of his place with regard, much tenderness and some irony. He is the understudy who mouths the lead's lines wordlessly while performing its gestures in a stage set of his own design. Watching from the wings, he is inside the theatre of place and yet stands just off-stage. From this vantage point, he fields the tensions between the outsider's objective gaze and the insider's subjective responses to a perceived reality. To borrow from the poet and critic Eli Mandel, Thauberger is ''a man not so much in place, as out of place and so endlessly trying to get back...'' This tension, which activates Thauberger's work, also gives it one of its most dis-

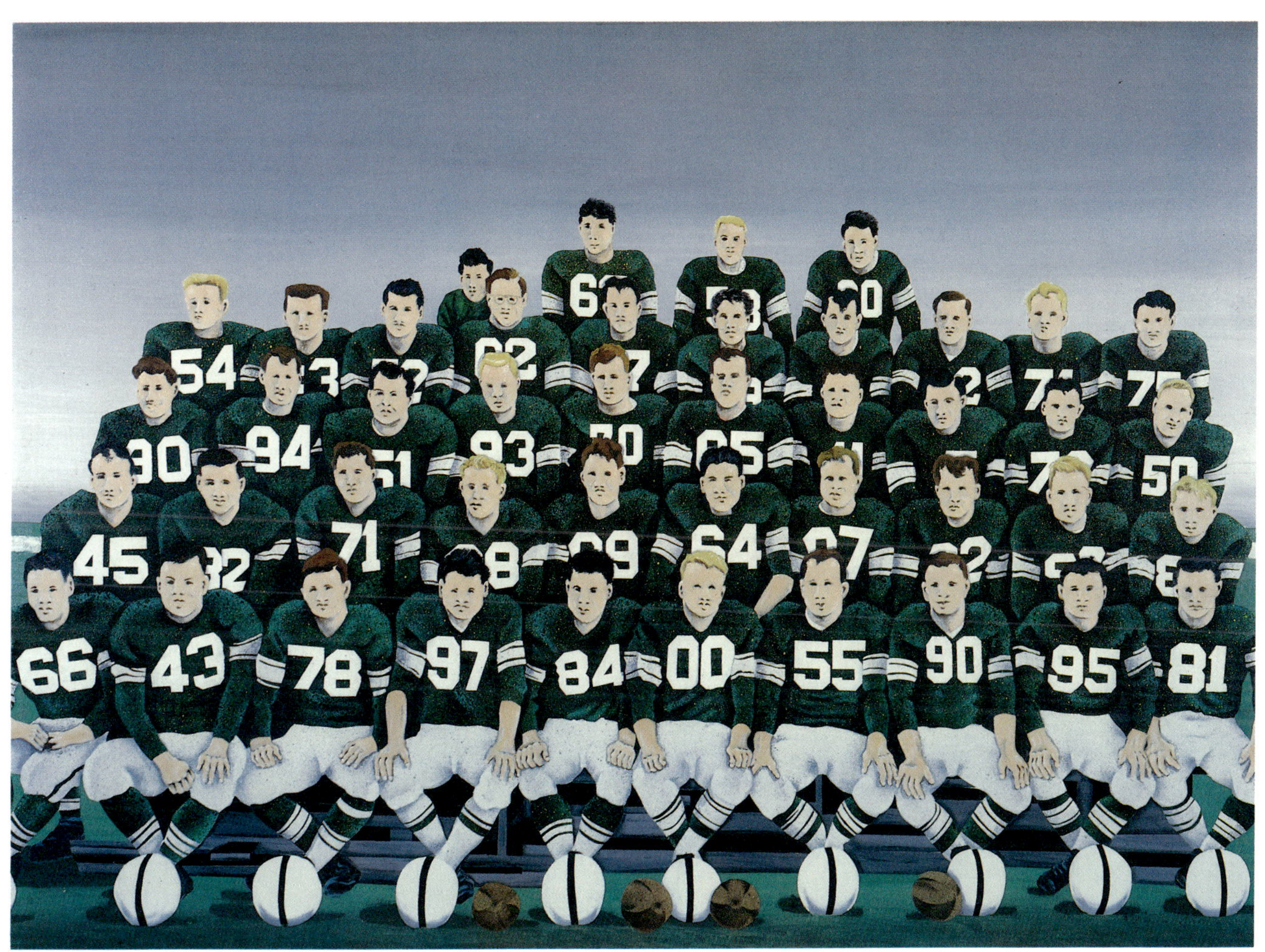

Plate 5 *Green and White Painting (Dobberville)* 1980 (cat. 12)

tinguishing characteristics. His insider's knowledge of culture's role provides the substance that weights his outsider's point of view and stays his hand at condescension. Living on the inside but working from the outside, he neither scorns nor satirizes manifestations of popular culture that other artists have found all too tempting targets. He heightens his sense of place by heightening what he understands to be the sensibilities of its grassroots community, but treats them both with equal esteem. At the same time, the tensions in his work keep to an edge that makes us think all is not harmonious in this local Arcadia, that culture — high or low — is a hedge against the void.

Such an existential possibility is not to be found in Thauberger's subject matter alone; the complexities and subtleties of his perspective on culture and place are inscribed in his style. This is where his double vision takes its physical and visual form. Always, we are made aware that Thauberger's vision of reality is perceived through the filter of culture, a filter with which he merges aspects of vernacular and popular culture and modernist art. In effect, he has created a visual style that corresponds to the poet or fiction writer's use of vernacular voice or speech, something that none of the other of his Saskatchewan colleagues have done in quite the same way. The achievement of this voice, animated with the tensions arising from the interplay of contradictory forms, resolved for him the contradictions between language and expression that he experienced in Regina as a student in the late 1960s. These contradictions have been described most eloquently by Saskatchewan writers; but the crux of the problem applies to visual artists in Saskatchewan as well.

For Thauberger, as for other prairie artists and writers, finding his voice and finding his place were synonymous. We might ask why he had to find his place when he was already there; the answer is that without speech, without a visual language in which to embody place and to express the culture of its folkways, he had no place and no articulated identity. Art and art teaching in Regina in the 1960s were dominated by an imported form of late modernist abstraction whose roots were in European and American modernism. From Thauberger's point of view, this was an empty formalist language without an immediate or relevant context to give it life or meaning. Art, in order to be authentic for him, had to be rooted in the specifics of lived experience that included not only who you were but also where you were, and did not try to separate identity from place. In order to make art, Thauberger had to put things in place, to return both literally and figuratively to his origins.

The elements of Thauberger's painting style began to coalesce after he returned to Regina in 1973, following two years of graduate study in the United States. As a painter, Thauberger is self-taught. His opposition to what he saw as a rigid, colonial version of modernist dogma in Regina painting led him to abort his initial attempt to study art. He was lured back by clay and the renegade attitudes of the California ceramic artist David Gilhooly, who taught at the University of Saskatchewan at Regina from 1969 to 1971. Studying under Gilhooly, whose irreverent Funk Art sculpture influenced him heavily (fig. 1), Thauberger completed a B.F.A. in 1971. He then took an M.A. at California State University in Sacramento in 1972 and an M.F.A. at the University of Montana in Missoula in 1973. All three degrees were in ceramics; but early in his California studies, Thauberger began to look at paintings for ideas and ways to solve pictorial problems in clay. In particular, the work of two California artists, William T. Wiley's pun-filled autobiographical fantasies (fig. 2) and Wayne Thiebaud's lush, iconic figures and foods (fig. 3), were a revelation. Their examples showed Thauberger how a painter might go about making art from the everyday images and textures of

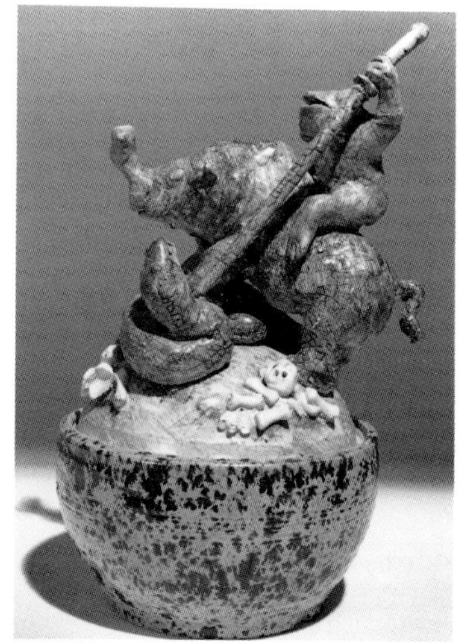

Fig. 1 David Gilhooly
St. George and the Dragon 1969
Clay, glaze and china paint
31.5 × 17.8 × 17.8 cm
Collection of David Thauberger

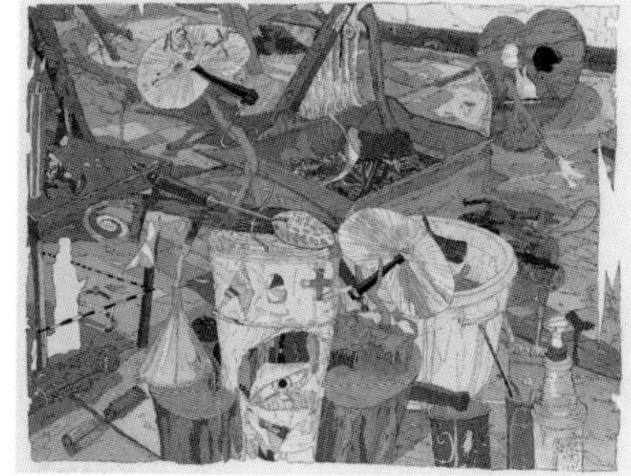

Fig. 2 William T. Wiley
Eerie Grotto Okini 1982
Woodcut
55.9 × 76.2 cm
Collection of David Thauberger

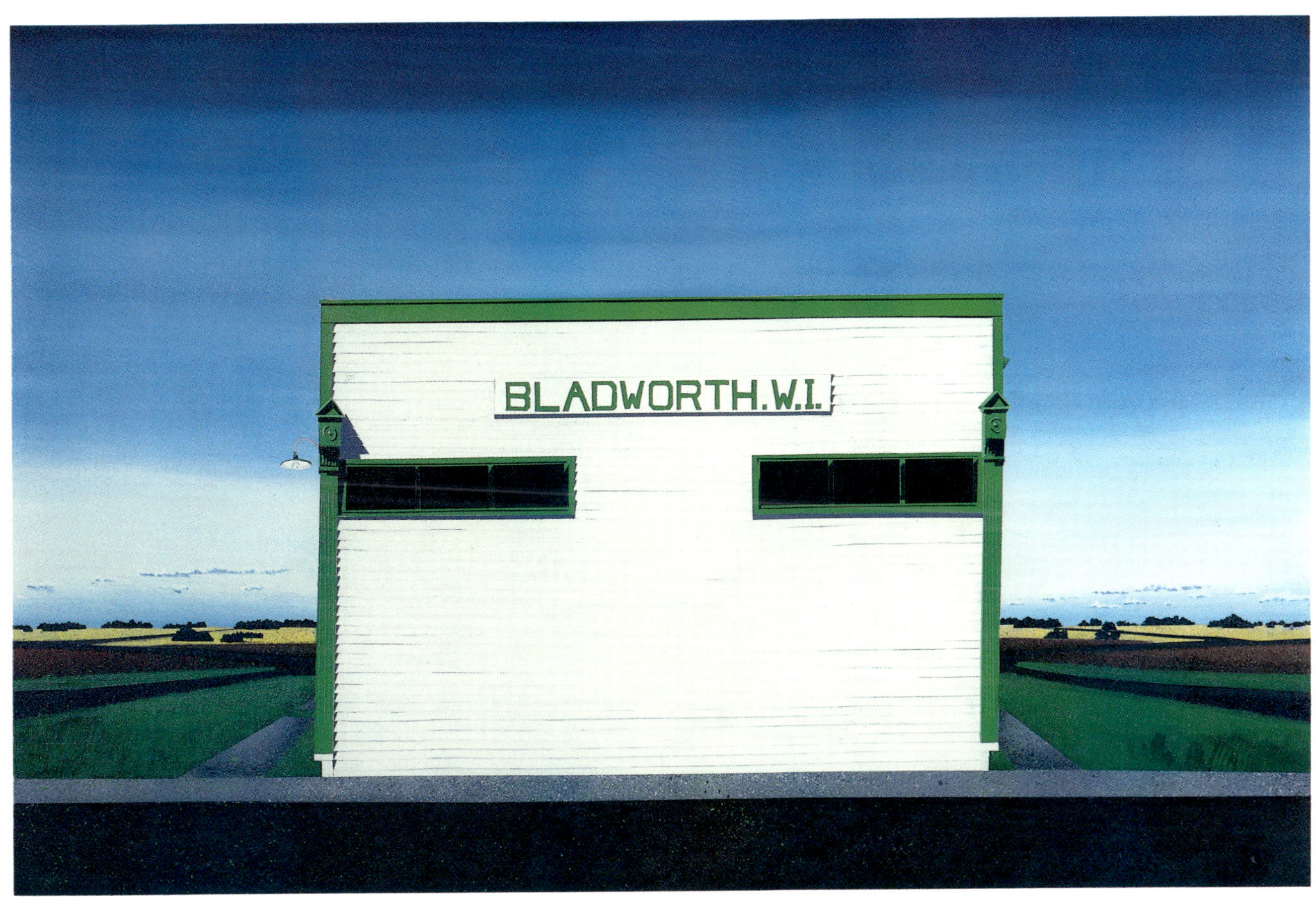

Plate 6 *Kachina* 1981 (cat. 14)

life in a specific cultural environment. Their work offered him formal direction as well, in Wiley's handling of watercolour and Thiebaud's construction of compositions. But these were only two prime factors in a complex equation of influences.

Thauberger soaked up a rich variety of art-making in California. Some of the ideas he encountered had first been introduced to him by Gilhooly's slide lectures in Regina. The array spread out around him as a graduate student included the work of ceramic sculptor Robert Arneson, painters Joseph Raffael and Roy De Forest, the Chicago Imagists Jim Nutt, Gladys Nilsson, Roger Brown (fig. 4) and Karl Wirsum, and the Chicago folk artist Joseph Yoakum. What attracted Thauberger to these artists was their insistence on personal imagery and subject matter, their attachment to place, their free formal invention, their openness to the vitality of popular and non-Western cultures, and their adversarial relationship to high-art modernist culture as dictated from New York. In this intense atmosphere, Thauberger began to teach himself to paint and, in the more contemplative space he created for himself in Montana, he became deeply immersed in painting. All the while, he continued to work as a sculptor in clay.

Resolving contradictions between pictorial ideas and sculptural forms was just one of the problems for Thauberger to solve when he went home to Regina. Most importantly, he had to find a way to bridge the gap between his experiences in the United States and the life he knew and discovered he wanted to portray in Saskatchewan. In order to find his own voice, he had to relocate himself in place, not only physically, but conceptually as well. For a while he floundered, working alternately in painting and clay to digest and absorb what he had learned. One of his major preoccupations during this transitional period was to incorporate motifs drawn from the local popular culture into his work in both painting and sculpture.

Working in clay, Thauberger built architectural and pictorial vignettes that included, with increasing frequency, found objects and recycled ceramics. To his own ceramic structures, he added such things as beer glasses, cups, salt and pepper shakers, small trophies, figurines and vases. The themes of these works focused on aspects of the local economy, bars, cars, motorcycle shops, service stations, supermarkets, local pastimes and folklore, and occasionally, the landscape. Much of this clay sculpture was broadly and self-consciously satirical in the manner of Funk Art. Thauberger's paintings, apart from a brief flirtation with Photorealism, took a more abstract and lyrical approach. In large-scale canvases, he constructed visually complex patterns of repeated images such as birds, animals and fish. Sometimes these patterns were superimposed like an openwork screen on a foreground plane over a distant landscape; the overall effect of the pattern being to intensify some quality of the scene beyond. At the same time, Thauberger was also experimenting on paper, working out what for painting were unorthodox techniques: flocking, stencilling and splatter rendering applied in watercolour with a toothbrush. The splatter technique was inspired by nineteenth-century lithographic illustrations in agricultural books and seed catalogues. But what he lacked for these experiments in content and form was a cohesive conceptual framework that would allow him to get past the surface of things to what mattered to him.

It was finally Saskatchewan's folk artists who provided Thauberger with the map to his place and the context for his vernacular style. Honest, direct and unself-consciously immersed in the particulars of their lives, surroundings and memories, the folk artists literally changed his perception of

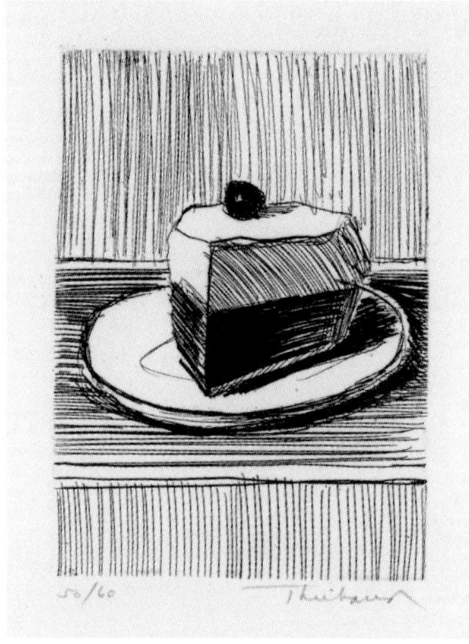

Fig. 3 Wayne Thiebaud
Pie Slice 1964
Etching
25.5 × 20.2 cm
Collection of David Thauberger

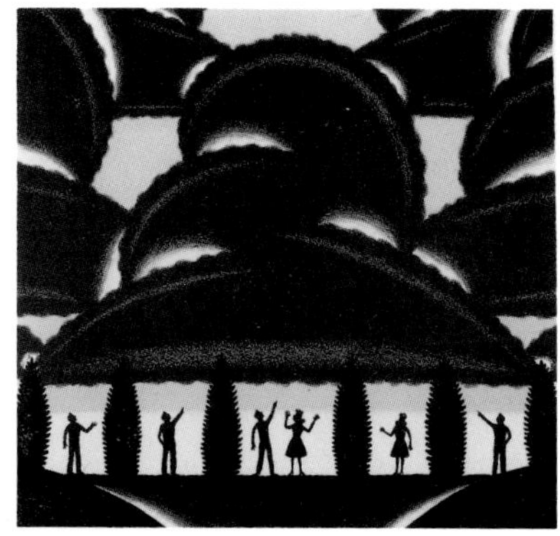

Fig. 4 Roger Brown
Little Nimbus 1979
Lithograph
25.3 × 26.7 cm
Collection of David Thauberger

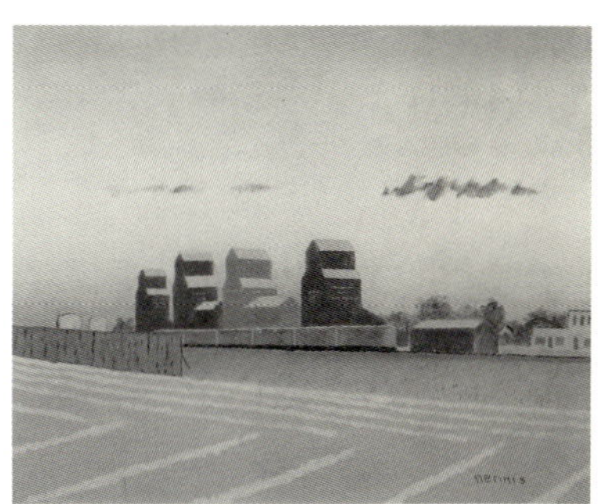

Fig. 5 Wesley Dennis
Four Elevators 1977
Oil on canvas mounted on board
40.3 × 51.1 cm
Collection of David Thauberger

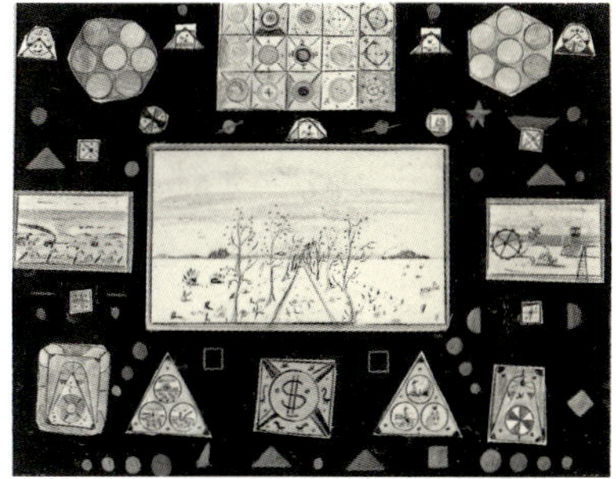

Fig. 6 W. C. McCargar
Untitled n.d.
Wax crayon, gouache, pencil crayon,
graphite pencil, ballpoint pen, marking
pen and glitter on paper with collage
20.6 × 25.9 cm
Collection of David Thauberger

place and how an inhabitant might function within it as an artist. Two men became Thauberger's mentors. One was Wesley Dennis of Brownlee, Saskatchewan, a retired farmer fifty years Thauberger's senior who, through the heightened lyrical vision of his landscape paintings, showed the younger artist a prairie setting he had grown up in but had never seen in such a way before (fig. 5). The other man, who became Thauberger's model of the isolated artist making art with an awareness of a larger world outside, was W. C. McCargar (fig. 6), a retired Canadian Pacific Railway station agent living in Regina. Thauberger discovered McCargar's work first, while he was cataloguing the art collection of the Saskatchewan Arts Board in 1974–75. He then sought out other folk artists like Wesley and Eva Dennis, who lived outside of the city in small towns. They were self-taught as he was self-taught as a painter; they drew ideas and images from popular culture as he did; they sought fresh inventive solutions to formal problems as he was doing. For Thauberger, the folk artists became the local manifestations of the attitudes and attachments he had found in the work of the artists he admired in California.

Significantly, the example of his folk artist colleagues also offered Thauberger a different tone of voice than that of the California and Chicago artists, one that was integral to *his* chosen place. The visual culture within which the folk artists lived and worked was one of local architecture and crafts, television, calendars, art reproductions, postcards, magazine photographs, illustrations, advertising of all kinds, greeting and trading cards, paintings on black velvet, all manner of kitsch, hobby kits, how-to books, etc. Dennis learned to paint by imitating reproductions; McCargar, after he was urged to give up his paint-by-number kits, looked to art books, reproductions and postcards. Thauberger had long used such sources in his own work. Yet Dennis, McCargar and other Saskatchewan folk artists surely must also have shown Thauberger how sources in popular and mass culture could be internalized, incorporated and transformed to create a higher level of expressive vocabulary.

The tone of folk art tends to elevate its popular source material, to pull it up rather than put it down. Folk art takes popular culture as the norm and high culture as the aberration worthy of ironic treatment. Thauberger also embraces the environment of popular culture as the real landscape of the everyday world. But he does this with the awareness that this landscape too has become permeated, over time, with the vocabulary of a popularized modernism. His vernacular tone thus achieves the synthesis that allows him to give voice in the same breath to the visual equivalents of dialect and cultured speech. He brings them together without archness or irony, but with an assertive emphasis on the vernacular that announces the merger as a calculatedly hybrid form, intent on declaring its difference.

We might speculate that not only Thauberger's tone of voice, but also his filtered vision came about as a result of his close contact with the folk artists. His first uses of glitter and flocking and other materials associated with folk art appear in the ceramic sculpture he made as a graduate student in California. At that time, the strategy seemed to be aimed at bringing his work into the iconoclastic sphere of Funk Art by emulating the broad category of kitsch — a phenomenon of low culture deemed to be valueless. Within the Saskatchewan context, however, such devices as glitter and flocking were identifiable signs of a specific cultural practice, folk art, which there was deemed to be culturally valuable. The tone of Thauberger's vernacular voice incorporated that sense

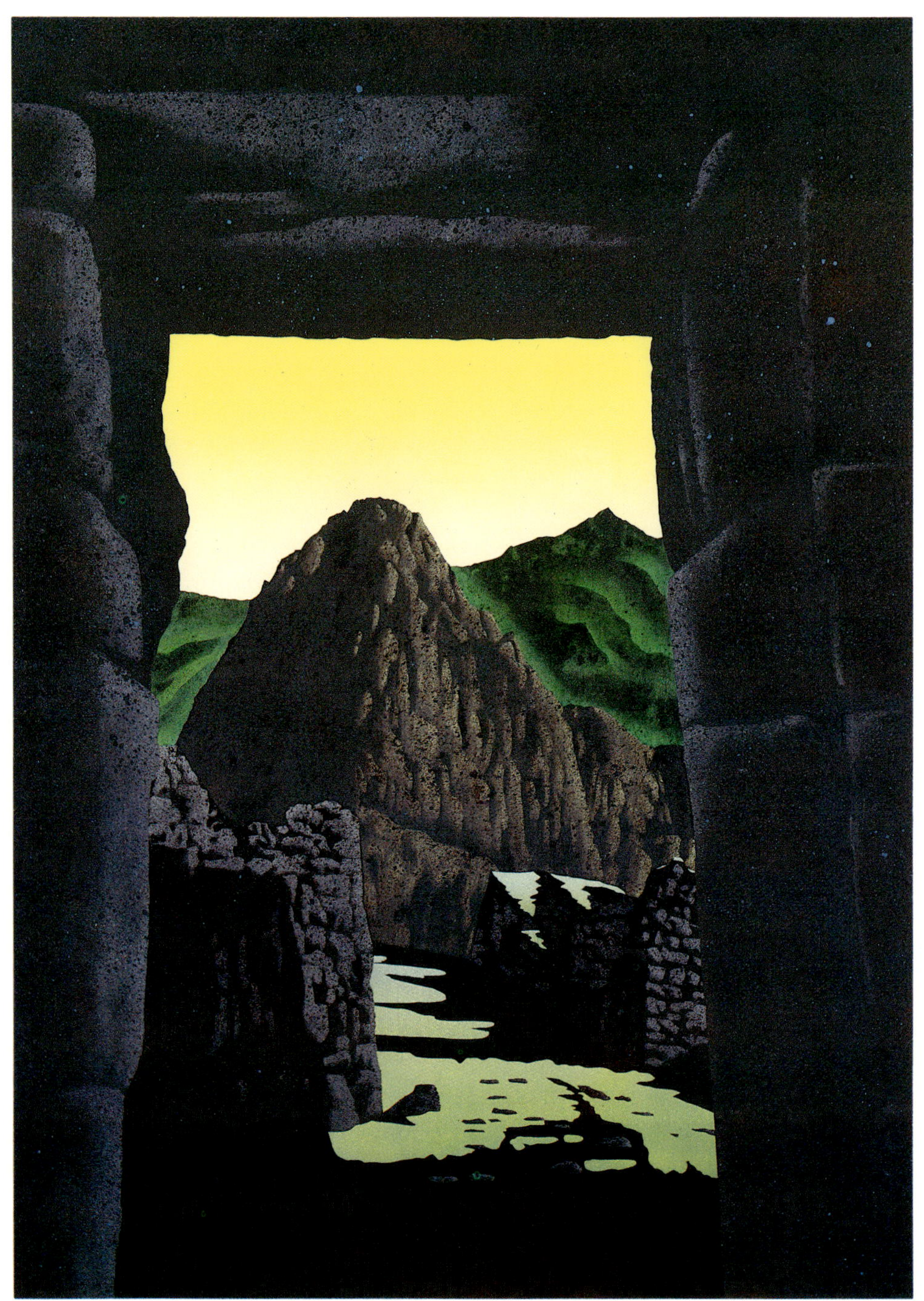

Plate 7 *Machu Picchu* 1984 (cat. 24)

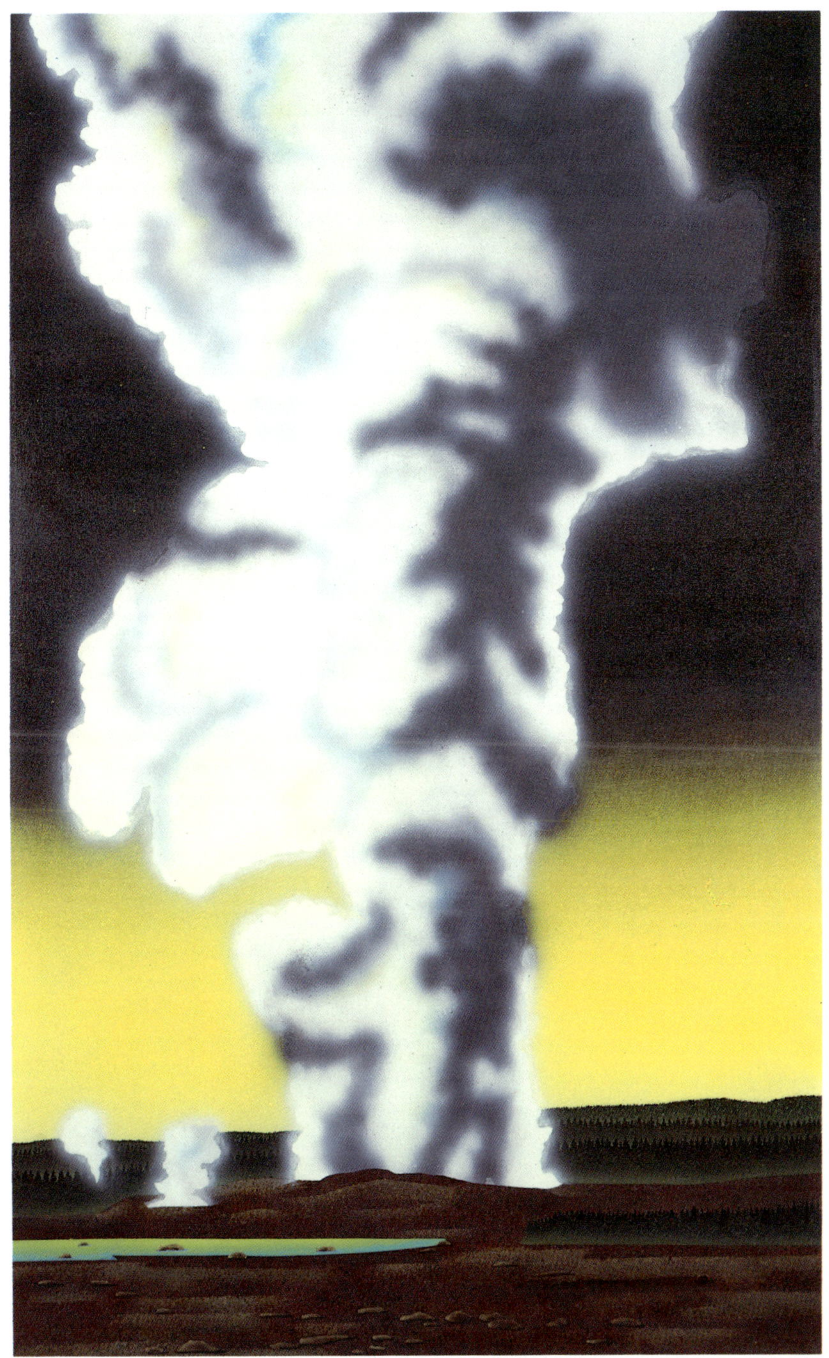

Plate 8 *Big Geyser* 1983 (cat. 20)

of value together with some of the folk artist's own values. Parallel to this ran his apparent recognition that a material or technique could function as a sign in painting, not only for folk art, but the entire culture of reproduced imagery as well. Be it an intuition or a by-product of Thauberger's kinship with the folk artists, this recognition might well have been the key that led him to develop his mature painting style in which images embody the culture from which they arise at the same time that they depict its milieu.

Two groups of works from the mid and late 1970s played significant roles in this development. Thauberger's last series of ceramic sculptures, made in 1975, portrayed false-front prairie buildings that either were or might have been the photographic subjects of postcards — *The Prince Charles* and *The Champ* hotels and *The Regal, The Grand* (fig. 7) and *The Roxy* movie theatres. So familiar as to be archetypes of prairie culture, they were part and parcel of Thauberger's origins. The ceramics led him to explore these origins more widely in 1977–78 through the images of small paintings, a series of watercolours of archetypal prairie buildings and landscapes that integrated splatter painting and stencilled patterns. In these paintings, Thauberger strove to make visible both the locus of an association and the nature of the association itself, by juxtaposing the representation of a building or scene with a related cultural sign. As in his earlier pattern paintings, he split the pictorial field vertically into two overlapping planes, with the foreground plane holding the pattern of repeated signs superimposed on the background image.

Now, however, Thauberger's motives were more conceptual than formal; he was beginning to establish a frame of reference for his portrayal of place, to relocate himself at home. He was looking at places filled with associations, at a place redolent with memories, and memory, at first, became the frame he held up to the culture. In *Danceland,* 1977, a grid of torpedo-back 1940s sedans appears parked across the hall's plain flat front; dancing movie-magazine couples fox trot across the Art Deco facade of *Roxy,* 1978 (fig. 8); and in another untitled watercolour of 1977, the see-through image of two huge confrontal chickens seems to have formed itself from the white clouds hovering over his grandfather's sun-washed farm house. However, the aura of nostalgia around these scenes, the sense that they are memory pictures, emanates less from the patterned images than from the splatter technique that Thauberger translated literally into painting from early forms of printing. The soft, layered textures of the splattered paint breaks the images into thousands of tiny coloured dots, reducing extraneous details and rendering forms with an illustrational simplicity.

This effect in the large canvases that follow the watercolours, such as the *Green and White Painting,* 1978 (pl. 9), and *Rainbow Danceland,* 1979, two acrylic and glitter paintings of dance halls, is like that of a theatrical scrim, which idealizes the scenes and holds them at several steps remove from the audience. In fact, the flat but softly modelled images appear to be as thin as scrim, illusions of colour and light projected on a sparkling blank screen. Three dancing couples float, like echoes of faint music, through the sky of *Green and White Painting;* the feathery fronds of off-stage plants frame *Rainbow Danceland.* But such locating devices are hardly needed any longer. Thauberger has fused into one the two separate planes of the splatter watercolours. This melting together comes about through the optical and physical performance of a technique whose myriad multi-coloured dots might refer as easily to the nineteenth-century reproductive lithography that inspired them as to the dot-screens of the modern offset lithography process or the particles of coloured light that

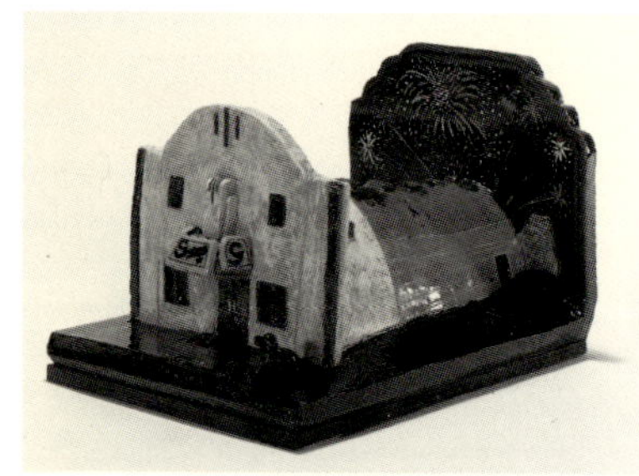

Fig. 7 *The Grand* 1975
Clay, glaze, acrylic and wood base
23.0 × 26.0 × 35.0 cm
Glenbow Museum, Calgary, Alberta

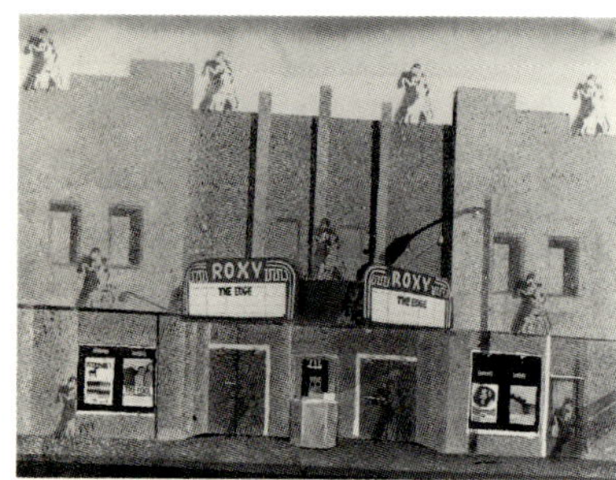

Fig. 8 *Roxy* 1978
Watercolour and acrylic on paper
65.1 × 83.0 cm
Private Collection

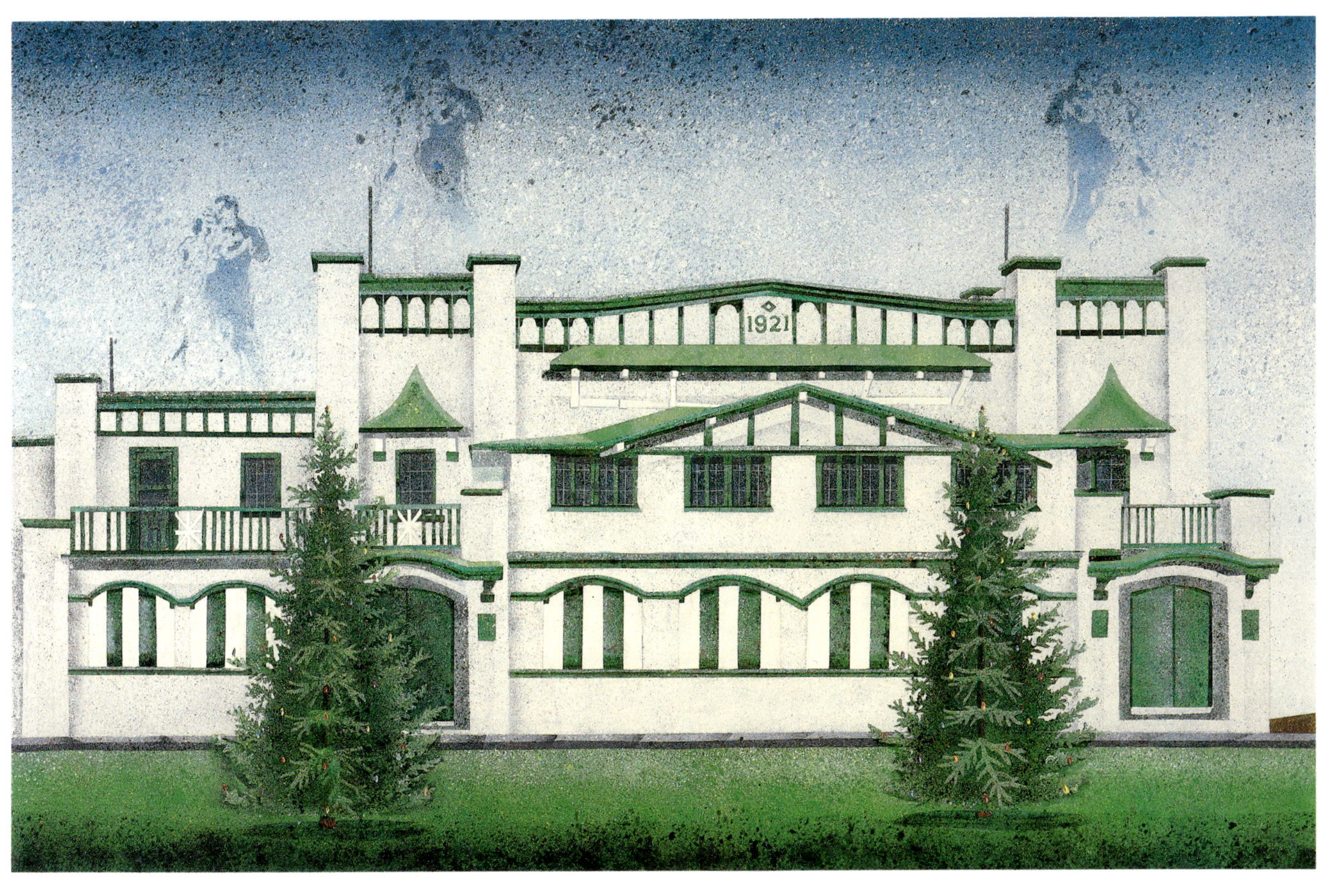

Plate 9 *Green and White Painting* 1978 (cat. 2)

form the images in a television screen. For as Thauberger imbues his images with their relationship to the common forms of reproduction pervading popular culture, facts and symbols merge into unified cultural signs. Each of Thauberger's images from 1978 onwards reflects his points of reference in popular culture; they become encoded by style in the unity of his vision.

If the splatter technique lays the ground of this rapport with mechanical reproduction in Thauberger's painting, it is built upon formally in several ways. Balanced against his extreme pictorial flatness and compression of space there are his illustrator's modelling and the collage-like skins of paint that accrue from his practice of masking and painting separately isolated areas of the canvas. Thauberger takes his vivid synthetic colours directly from the tubes and exploits their chemical hues to create often dissonant or edgy colour relationships. He cultivates an artificial naturalism. His compositions mime the branches of a family tree that is rooted as firmly in the picture postcard view, the standard frontal architectural photograph, the calendar landscape, the magazine illustration or photographic genre from the picture press as it is in Pop Art, Post-Impressionism, the paintings of Wayne Thiebaud or Japanese colour woodblock prints of the Edo period. Even the way Thauberger works as he tapes and untapes the canvas field, building images in layers and adjacencies, suggests the screening processes of printing. His process itself is both abstract and physical — most of the elements of an image must be pre-visualized before he begins a painting. He reproduces the image he holds in his mind, seeing its physical manifestation only when the last bits of tape are pulled away.

At the same time that the photographic source always lies just behind a Thauberger image, he makes us constantly aware of the actions of his hands and the physical nature of the painting as an object. Untaped edges are left ragged and escaping drips fall where they may; the way a painting was made reads as a subtext of the images. Glitter adds not only a reference to the greeting card or the work of W. C. McCargar but also light to colour and texture to the surface of a form. Thin skins of paint are textured, overlapped and layered to stand as physical equivalents of the thing represented and to provoke the sensation of being in its presence. Objects adhered to the surface of a canvas, like the drills bits on *Black Rain,* 1985 (fig. 9), or the spiral nails on *Some Acid Rain,* 1985 (pl. 17), which signify the sting of needle-sharp rain on skin or the pitting action of acid on the Parthenon's marble, operate as textures, patterns and metaphors. And aspenite, a textured board Thauberger used as the support of a group of postcard-inspired landscape paintings, leaves an ironic echo of Cézanne's brushstroke in *the rocky mtns,* 1982 (pl. 20). But when all is said and done, Thauberger's work emphatically states that all of this is illusion, that whatever feelings these works might engender arise from a response to an illusion. The paradox is that for Thauberger and for many of his viewers, the feelings are real.

The surfaces of Thauberger's paintings represent the antithesis of the anonymous finish of the photo-mechanical reproduction; in them, he seeks the wellspring of feeling rising in the images and the authenticity of painting inherent in the handmade object. We might equate this authenticity with the authenticity of vernacular voice and a rooted existence in place and community. By the same token, Thauberger's stylistic synthesis and references keep us mindful of the power of ephemera and the ways in which photo-mechanical reproductions effect our perceptions of a changing world. By incorporating references to reproduction in his style, Thauberger also embodies con-

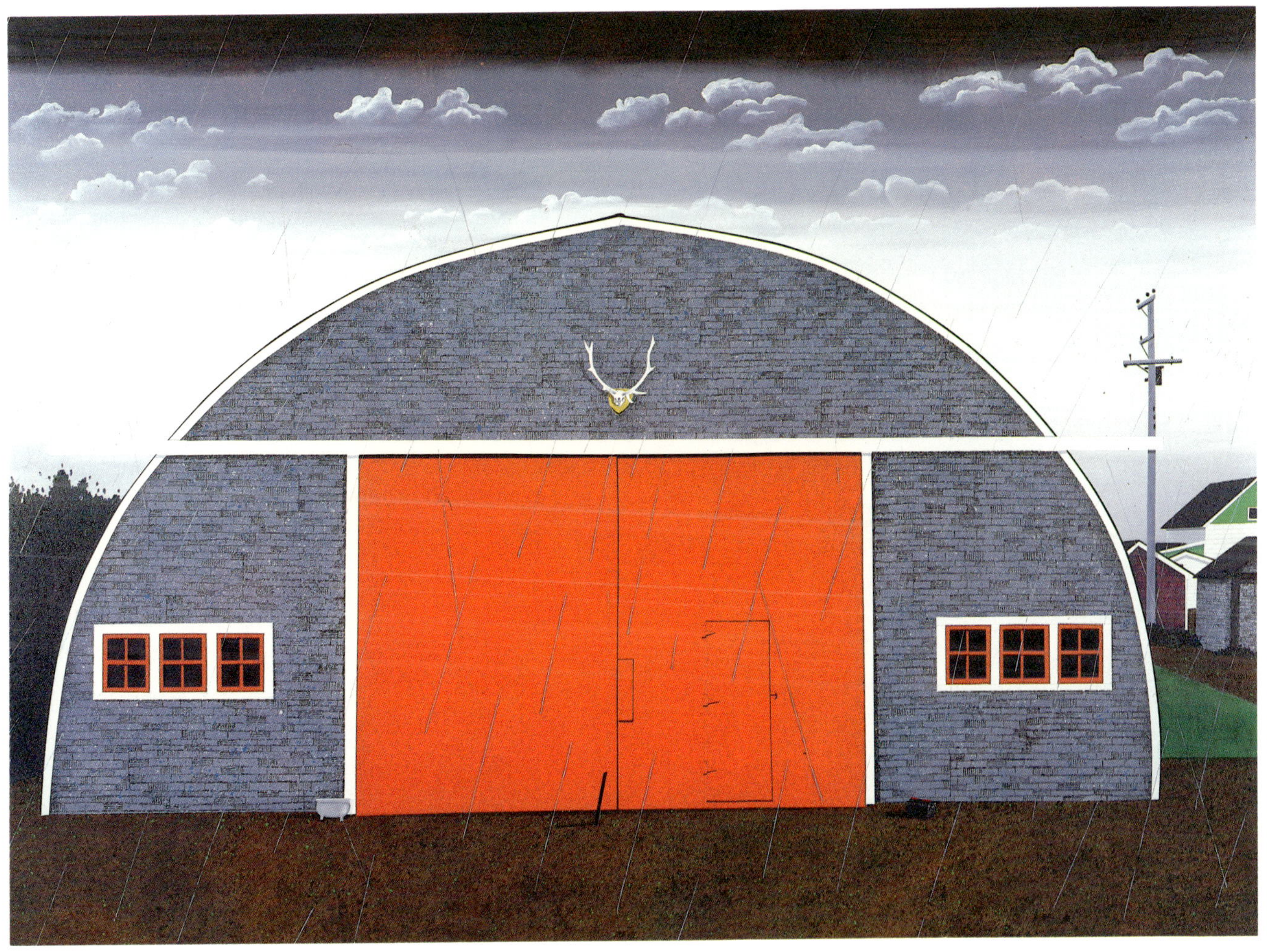

Plate 10 *Light Shower* 1981 (cat. 15)

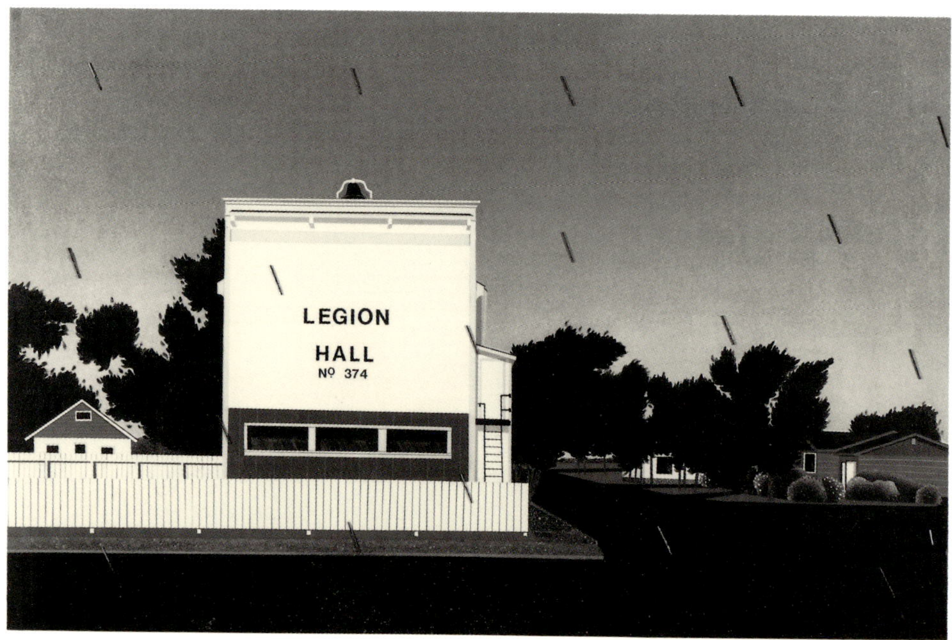

Fig. 9 *Black Rain* 1985 (cat. 25)

traditions in the content of his paintings. If we can sense the presence of the photograph behind Thauberger's images, we can also sense, as well as see, the prairie false-front facade. Something in the nature of the grassroots Depression intuition that 'things are too good to be true' also lies behind these images, even when Thauberger's prairie community, with its rural roots, small towns, cities and suburbias, seems to be a midwestern Arcadia.

The facade, the screen, the screened image becomes a metaphor that projects the ideal and its opposite at the same time. Thauberger's images are images about other absent images whose harmony, order and beauty lie in the eye of the beholder. His paintings are full and hauntingly empty at the same time, both permanent and transient, as though the soft dot-screens might dissolve and the thin collages of paint revolve to show their other sides. A void, however romantically tinted by sunsets, dawn, a sudden shower, or mid-afternoon sun, yawns behind the building that presents its sturdy front. But this intimation in Thauberger's work seems less like pessimism than a hard-headed prairie poetics, one which acknowledges the facts within the symbols, and the fact that places, the people who build communities, and the cycles of life are always and inevitably on the brink of change. There is always poignance in the ideal; Thauberger incorporates this in the synthesis of his work.

David Thauberger is very much a man of his own place and times. When he went home to Regina in 1973, he returned to a different place than the one he had left, one he came to see through different eyes. The beginnings of his vernacular style were framed by memory and personal history in the large acrylic paintings of 1978–79. Though tied to a collective cultural memory, even his painting of the Crystal Palace was related to a personal event, his first trip to Europe to look at art; he was bringing his adventures back home. His first large prarie landscapes of this period — *Night Lilies, Slough* and *Harvest Painting* (pls. 14–16) — were in part homage to painters who had influenced him: Monet, Joseph Raffael, Wesley Dennis. But by 1980–81, Thauberger's internalized focus had begun to move outward, expanding to encompass and magnify more and more of place itself. In two years, after much experimentation, he had set the themes and stylistic course of his major work. He had established the coordinates of place at the centre of an axis aligned between the local and the cosmopolitan, the everyday and the exotic, the material and the existential worlds, the reproduction's idealized reality and the reality of painting.

Any locale reached by mass communications in the contemporary world is the meeting place of vernacular, popular, modernist and mass cultures. Thauberger's achievement is grounded in the ways he has recognized and acknowledged this. In effect, he has constructed a place and turned it inside out. Coming full circle, his largest subject is regionalism itself. Thauberger's most recent screenprint, *Farm Yard,* 1987 (fig. 10), makes this statement with precision and economy. The print shows a sophisticated image as simple as a pastoral postcard scene. With minimal means, it depicts an ample red barn in the foreground, a crisp white farmhouse — his grandfather's house — in the middle distance and, beyond them, golden fields of stooks under a vast prairie sky. The image is as thin as ink and covered all over with the dots of a half-tone screen enlarged to a scale that can be seen clearly. If there were a message on the verso, it might read: "Wish you were here."

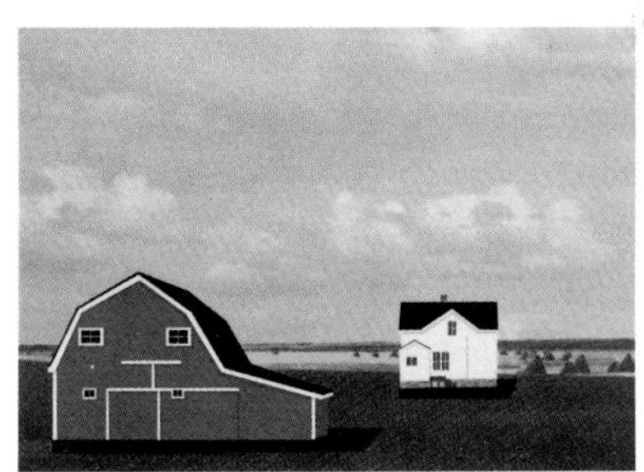

Fig. 10 *Farm Yard* 1987
Screenprint
37.7 × 53.2 cm

1. Michel Nedjar, "I Am Tied to the Threads of the World," assembled and translated by Roger Cardinal, in *Art Brut: Madness and Marginalia,* edited by Allen S. Weiss, special issue, *Art & Text* 27 (December 1987—February 1988), p. 58.

2. Saskatchewan poet and critic Dennis Cooley discusses the roots and connotations of the terms region and local in "The Vernacular Muse in Prairie Poetry," in *The Vernacular Muse: The Eye and Ear in Contemporary Literature* (Winnipeg: Turnstone Press, 1987), p. 209. The distinctions he makes are useful to consider here. Quoting Foucault on "the military bases" of terms such as region and province, Cooley goes on to suggest that the terms come to designate "subjugation" and "cultural bullying" and the imposition of a cultural "standard" from the outside. In the term local, he finds more positive connotations: "it refers to a rooted existence, one that stands in contrast to the deracinated perspective of centralists and 'cosmopolitans.'"

3. Flannery O'Connor, "The Regional Writer," in *Flannery O'Connor — Mystery and Manners: Occasional Prose,* selected and edited by Sally and Robert Fitzgerald (New York: Farrar, Straus & Giroux, 1961), p. 57.

4. The structure represented in *Crystal Palace* is actually the Great Palm House at Kew, built from 1844 to 1848.

5. Marshall Berman, *All That is Solid Melts into Air: The Experience of Modernity* (Harmondsworth: Penguin Books, 1988), pp. 235–36.

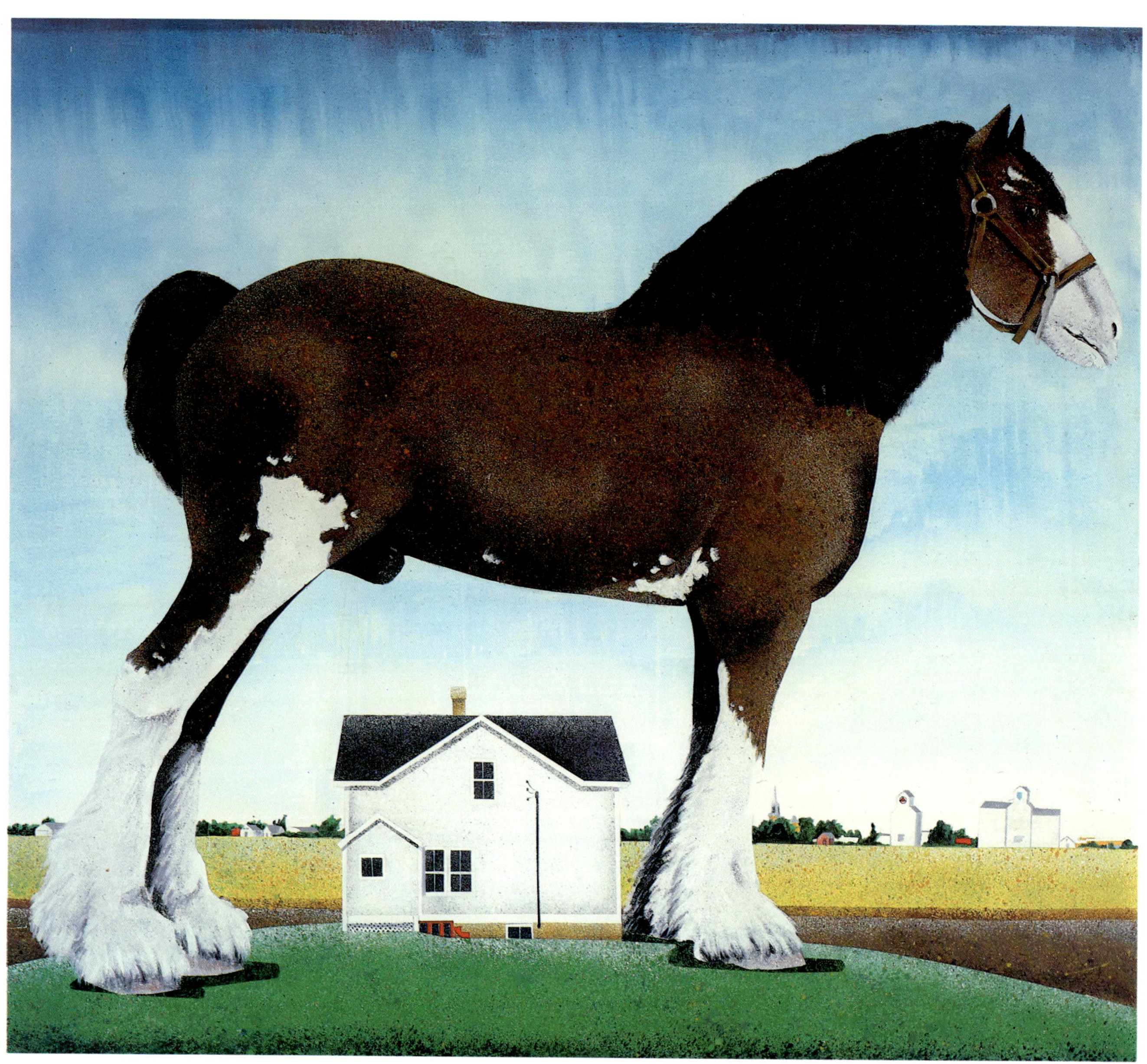

Plate 11 *Grandfather's Painting* 1978 (cat. 1)

DAVID THAUBERGER'S PAINTINGS: POPULAR MYTHS/CULTURAL REALITIES

Peter White

In a paper presented in 1979 to the Saskatchewan Library Association, the poet and critic Eli Mandel made a case for a fundamental change of cultural sensibility involving notions of academic and popular.[1] What has been considered high or official culture, Mandel argued, has lost relevance; the ground historically occupied by high art has been invaded by a sensibility, both anti-literary and anti-humanist, that is responsive to mass culture. Referring to Leonard Cohen's *Beautiful Losers* in the context of that complex and often obscure work's widespread appeal, Mandel wrote, ''Art has become popular, not academic. Its field of reference was no longer the tradition of human letters but the imagery, style, and content of mass culture itself and it now served not the humanist tradition but the values of the new culture.''

Part of the fascination, as well as the challenge, of Mandel's discussion is that while it arises from a tension between high art and mass culture, it does not simply polarize these terms. Mandel does not contend, for example, that the role of high culture has somehow been or should be replaced by an open embrace of popular culture, a situation that would only reinforce their traditional opposition. Rather, the crux of the issue is that in contemporary society what matters is taking place at a popular and mass cultural level. In this there is a relationship to Pop Art but with the important distinction that the situation Mandel outlines goes beyond the ironic distance or the often barely repressed fetishism of high art looking to, valorizing, or simply inhabiting the forms of popular expression. In effect, the forms of high or academic art have not only been reconciled to the world around them but have themselves become means of popular expression. ''*The classroom reality has become popular;* it is the home of mass culture.''[2]

The implications of such developments are far reaching, most directly for conceptions of what constitutes literacy and art but, more widely, for radical changes across the whole spectrum of society with political, sociological and historical significance. In fact, it may be questioned whether actual change has been quite as profound as Mandel infers. However transformed or its context redefined, the centrality of art remains with many of its traditional and distinctive values intact. Yet perhaps what is more important — and indeed this is what Mandel seems to have in mind — is that such altered perception or sensibility embodies a fluid and evolving new context in which traditional cultural formations and structures, most evidently high-low/academic-popular hierarchies, are placed under pressures that open the way to more self-critical, meaningful and, for Mandel, socially necessary cultural and social definitions.

Mandel's analysis, itself responsive to what was then the emergent model of postmodern culture, is developed from an awareness of the vast technological developments that have increasingly affected experience through new forms of communications and knowledge and intensified patterns of production, consumption and distribution. Mandel finds the purist and elitist values of modernism, their unifying and centralizing impulses, their standards and certainty, incapable of addressing this environment. They have become, he says, ''shabby.'' On the other hand, he doesn't see the technology that generated this environment as an answer. Instead, he proposes both refusal of false orders, false or pre-conceived structures and acceptance of chaos or, at least, learning to live with it. In language, Mandel associates chaos with process, deconstruction, flux, paradox and self-reflexive forms rather than timeless structures that exist outside works of art. Moreover, in one of those strange and wonderful leaps that distinguishes his thinking, Mandel equates such "destructive poetics" with regionalism.[3]

Mandel, a native of Estevan, Saskatchewan, who has spent most of his adult life in central Canada, has been one of this country's most provocative and sensitive critics on the subject of regionalism. One of the earliest and most important cases against the conception of regionalism as a reflection of a particular geography was his argument that regionalism is foremost a matter of origins: a myth or state of mind related to childhood accompanied by overpowering feelings of nostalgia.[4] In this subsequent consideration of the subject, Mandel again challenges passive or reactive connotations that are conventionally associated with regionalism. The aggressive and demanding forms that characterize contemporary regional expression in Canada, he argues, reflect a breakdown of traditional cultural patterns focused on the goal of national unity. In a post-national environment, culture aligns itself with local and regional interests.[5] And, while the familiar tensions between region and metropolitan centre, between local and national values, are sustained, these frictions are subsumed within a larger, global environment of which the contemporary region is a part and with which it interacts in the process of defining itself.

Something of what Mandel has in mind is apparent in a poem inspired by David Thauberger's *Grandfather's Painting,* 1978 (pl. 11).[6] Mandel acquired the painting during his tenure as Writer-In-Residence at the Regina Public Library in 1978–79, the same period, not coincidentally, that he addressed the Saskatchewan librarians. The poem is structured by correlations between the painting and the film *Marathon Man* that Mandel finds himself watching on the Saturday night television movie. The painting is an expression of Thauberger's memories of growing up in rural Saskatchewan presented through the dramatic, sentinel-like figure of a horse that stands over the family farm house. The film is a Hollywood potboiler about "politics, betrayal and South American Nazis." Initially, the reality of Thauberger's remembered Saskatchewan pales beside what the film depicts, an overwhelming evil that is part of a demoralizing, larger pattern of evil that leads Mandel to question not only why he has returned to Saskatchewan but perhaps his continuing emotional attachment to it. Yet in due course the two realities are brought to some equivalence. The painting may be real as memory or myth, but it is only one version of reality. Things like "terrible forces" are not limited to the outside world. They are "inside us," Mandel concludes, in Thauberger's Saskatchewan as elsewhere.

"Grandfather's Painting: David Thauberger" is a disturbing poem. Yet in a regional context its almost bitter edge and lack of sentimentality within a sentimental structure of memory, reflection, confession and autobiography is a tonic to the reassuring nostalgia commonly associated with place. Moreover, place is not isolated. Indeed, it is thoroughly integrated into a comprehensive structure, one realized with great vividness by Mandel's pulp images of evil as they are viewed, "very small and peculiar," in the cold, dark loneliness of a prairie winter night. Referring to the images emanating from his television screen, Mandel says, "the real powers that run us" are "pictures." Most emphatically, these pictures, representations through which the world is experienced and understood, are popular images. And, although Mandel doesn't press the point, as the region and the larger world are related through the dark forces they share, Thauberger's painting can also be seen in terms of pictures. Its colossal figure refers to and belongs to an iconographic tradition that not

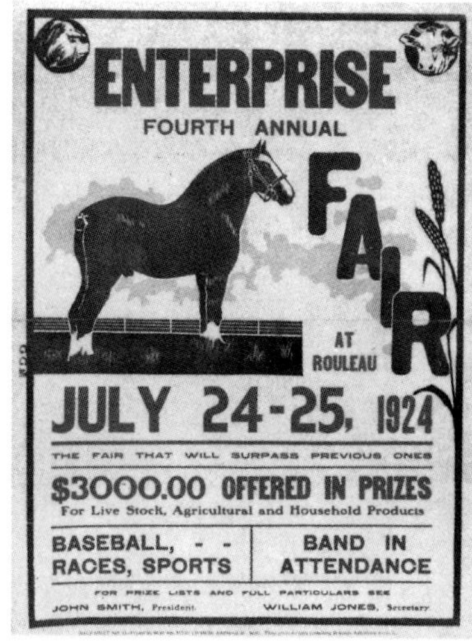

Fig. 11 Designer Unknown
Enterprise Fourth Annual Fair
Colour woodblock poster 1924
69.8 × 53.1 cm
Al and Shirley Fairground Collection,
Toronto

only goes back to antiquity but, in modern times, has had a particular presence in rural experience through photo-mechanical reproduction — posters, calendars and other graphic imagery (fig. 11) — and a genre of oversized popular and folk statuary motivated by concerns ranging from patriotism and civic pride to unsullied commercialism.[7] That a common, stock image is utilized to evoke the sense of a particular place is perhaps less ironic than it is simply appropriate. Indeed, it would seem the impact of the painting is largely dependent upon the familiar aura of its monumental, central motif.

Mandel's responsiveness to *Grandfather's Painting* is not surprising. Tinged with emotion and nostalgia, it is a forceful and memorable instance of his own understanding of regionalism as the memory of childhood. Yet the painting goes beyond what, for the regionalist perspective, is a crucial relationship to the past. Indeed, it participates in a conscious and determined manner in the kind of cultural concerns and strategies to which Mandel's criticism addresses itself. Whether or not its language could be described as a destructive poetics, *Grandfather's Painting* is certainly hostile to the refinement and purity associated with the late modernist object. Formally, it tends to the blatant. It also revels in its processes. The painting is highlighted with glitter; the colours of its acrylic paint, thin and loosely applied, in places splattered, are sharp if not jarring; its frame is painted; some of its underdrawing shows through; the ridged edges where areas were marked off with masking tape are clearly apparent. As well, with the flattening of its strongly profiled central image, the painting would seem to relate as much to its heritage of commercial graphics as it does to art. Reaching back in memory, Thauberger may have created an idealized and thoroughly coherent image. Nonetheless, as its undisguised lineage suggests, the image is thoroughly reflexive, presented both assertively and sensitively as part of a culture and tradition that is essentially popular and anti-elitist.

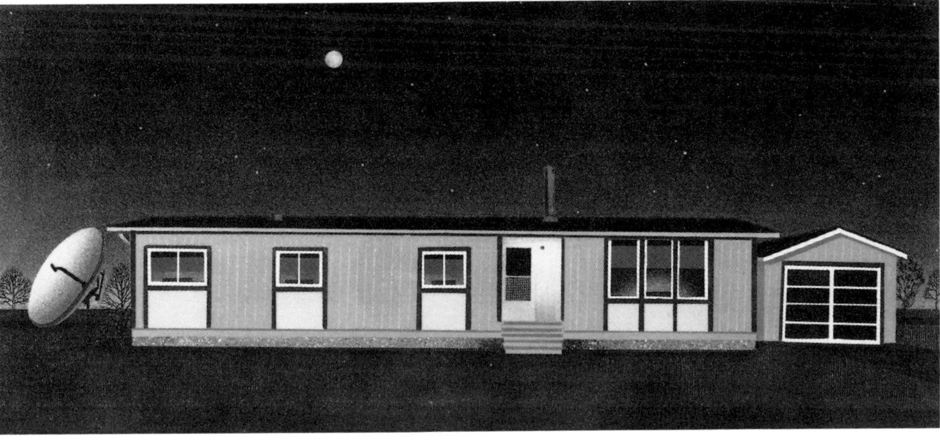

Fig. 12 *Motel — 24 Channels* 1985 (cat. 28)

With his appreciation of television, Mandel would no doubt also find much to consider in a more recent Thauberger painting. A small and otherwise modest work, *Motel — 24 Channels,* 1985 (fig. 12), depicts a nondescript, pre-fabricated structure that stands alone beneath a full moon on the open prairie. At one end of the building, pointed into the deep night sky, is a satellite dish, a technology that in recent years has not only hastened the onslaught of pictures but, in penetrating even the most isolated places, can be seen to represent the dynamics of an increasingly profound and complex relationship between the region and the larger mass culture. If Thauberger's massive horse served as an icon of the prairie past, this satellite dish is its present-day complement, symbol of a contemporary reality that is equally and vitally a part of the regionalist equation.

•

Thauberger has characterized his art as a process of coming to terms with place.[8] That process began in the late 1960s and early 1970s through a strongly felt aversion to modernism in its late and rarified form. Spurred by ongoing contact with the critic Clement Greenberg, for more than ten years formalist abstraction had been a predominant force in the visual arts in Regina.[9] As it was for many artists at this time, Thauberger's difficulties with this version of modernism stemmed from its irrelevance to his own life and interests. As one critic has suggested in connection with modernist autonomy, it forever runs the risk of cutting the subject off from his own history, "the fluidity of his own experience."[10] But it was also a question of attitude. Certain of its own historical correctness and inevitability, Greenbergian modernism not only lacked humour and flexibility, but it carried an offensive and not always disguised tone of condescension, if not contempt, for other points of view. With respect to the particular Saskatchewan context, what was presented as an appeal to universal values could as easily be seen in terms of the unsympathetic and often outright insensitive attitudes of distant urban centres — politically, economically as well as culturally dominant — towards rural-based peoples and societies.[11]

An important initial influence, as well as a continuing interest, was California Funk Art and Chicago Imagism. Thauberger was exposed to this work in Regina through the California ceramic sculptor David Gilhooly and subsequently during two years of graduate study in the United States in Sacramento and Montana. While absorbed and delighted by its humour and feeling for popular, commercial culture, Thauberger never embraced the more strident, irreverent or often hysterical tone that characterized much of that work.[12] A critical factor was his deep involvement with Saskatchewan's folk artists. In addition to their formal inventiveness, grounded in the lowbrow materials and imagery of mass culture, and the directness and emotional honesty with which they worked, Thauberger found himself inspired by the sophistication and moving commitment of these artists. From his perspective, the work involved relationships to place and the past rooted in an active concern with the present rather than, as is often claimed, a sentimental retreat from it. Folk art demonstrated that significant art not only can but, for him at least, must be based on where you are.

The most apparent reflection of Thauberger's regional identification has been his depiction of the distinctive architecture of Regina and the surrounding southern Saskatchewan grain belt — the false front commercial buildings of the small towns, the neat, "California-style" bungalows of the inner neighbourhoods of the larger centres, the appealing vernacular realizations of standard domestic and ecclesiastic building types. Images of enhancement, these carefully and lovingly constructed representations build an idea of this culture by dealing not simply with the look of the place but its emotional feel. Partly this is a matter of choosing representative buildings. But it also

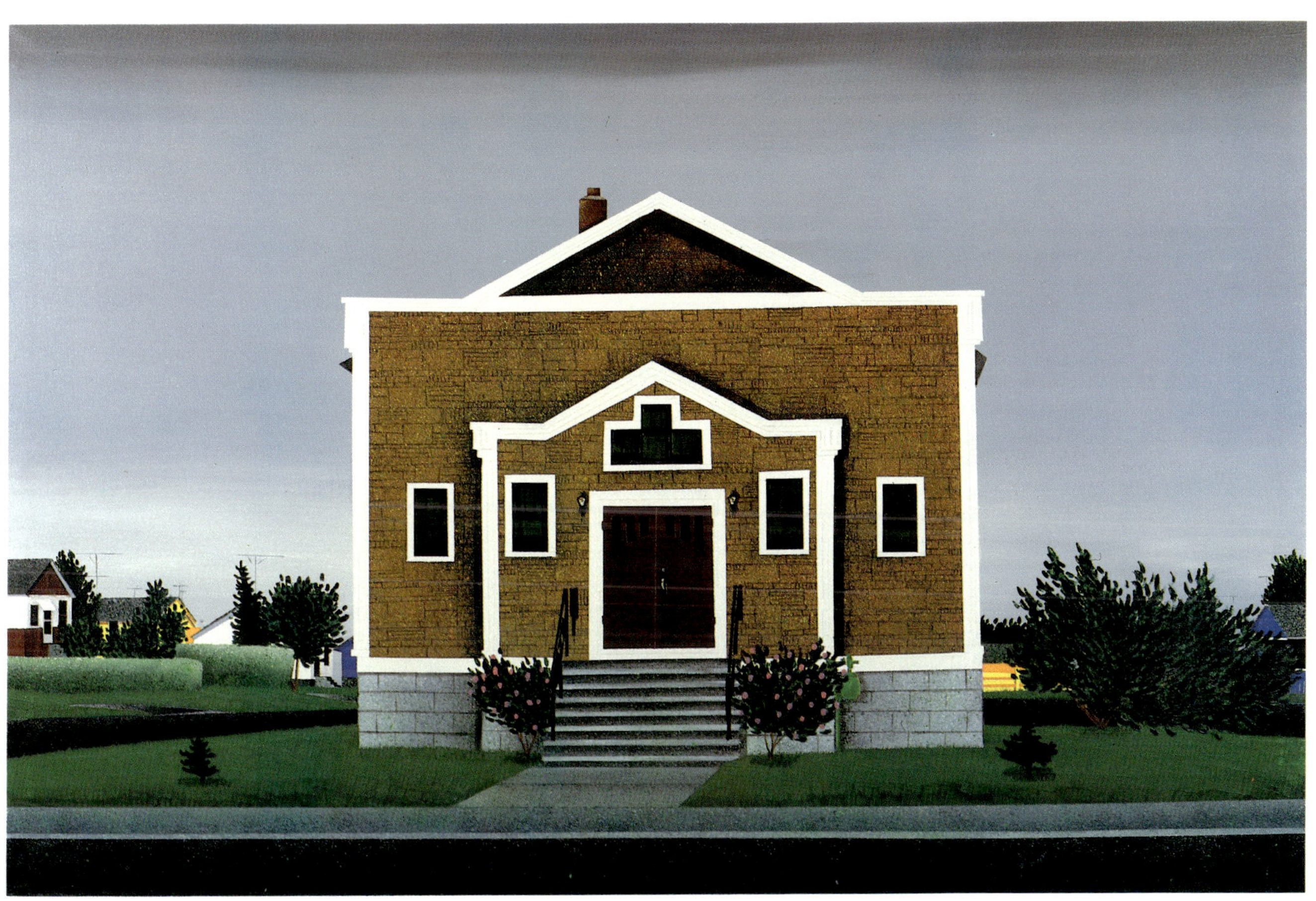

Plate 12 *Grey Painting* 1980 (cat. 13)

involves the perceptive observation of their particular visual logic and detail. For example, the facades of the small-town buildings are presented not in terms of some humble expedience but, rather, as integral, two-dimensional surfaces for the elaboration of beautifully concise decorative schemes. The emphatic frontality and intensified formal means used in the representation of these structures establish a presence that is both strong and memorable, especially when considered in relation to their exposure on the flat, open prairie. Symbolically, such presence relates to identity, which is understood as resilient and, equally important, assertive and positive.[13]

If Thauberger has concentrated on characteristic specifics of place, he has also situated this environment in a larger framework. This was true virtually from the time he committed himself to regional themes and issues in his paintings. A case in point is a cycle of large works from 1979 that includes *Crystal Palace, Night Lilies, Slough* and *Harvest* (pls. 13–16). The series begins with the Crystal Palace, the epitome of Victorian glasshouse architecture, an artificial paradise seen here as the home of exotic plants and flowers that include water lilies like those pictured in *Night Lilies*.[14] From this close-up view, with its sensuality and allusions to Monet, the theme is then transposed to the prairies, where these lilies appear in a slough, a marshy pond common to this part of the West. Finally, what began in the precious and controlled hothouse environment of early modern European culture concludes in a landscape that is presented as no less fantastic, a golden prairie wheat field at harvest time. Methodologically, these paintings relate to Mandel's approach, where consideration of prairie themes involved the generation of meaning by focusing on the common ground of seemingly disparate forms of experience. In these works, Thauberger not only makes a claim for the prairies as a subject matter worthy of great art, but he establishes a rich thematic continuum, extending in time and space, in which the prairies are seen in relation to, rather than isolated from, the social and economic developments and culture of their times.

A major pre-occupation of these paintings is the nature, fluidity and pervasiveness of culture. No matter how distinctive experience may be — in Thauberger's case personal or regional — when a direct line can be established that links the Crystal Palace to a prairie wheatfield, it is evident to what extent and with what power culture operates in the formation of reality. In a perhaps more obvious but nonetheless revealing series, Thauberger directed this line of inquiry to classical architecture, examining its permutations from its ancient origins, represented in *Some Acid Rain,* 1985 (pl. 17), by the Parthenon, through to its contemporary provincial echoes, in this case a wood-construction, small-town prairie Masonic Hall, *Intermittent Shower,* 1985 (pl. 18). The twist here, one that compounds the rather more straightforward observation of cultural genealogy, is the acid rain. Even the Parthenon, fountainhead of tradition, is not immune to what has become the tradition of a culture it spawned. Likewise, the question is raised whether the prairies, despite geographical isolation, can be isolated from such encroachments.

Beginning with the Crystal Palace cycle, much of Thauberger's concern with culture has taken the form of a response to and an assessment of modernity as a social experience. Constructed for the Great International Exposition of 1851 in London, the Crystal Palace itself is a modernist landmark. With its light, its transparency and its seemingly weightless construction, the building was a potent symbol of progress, an expression of faith in technology's capacity to deliver social betterment and individual well-being. In this context, the lilies can be seen as a sign of that well-being,

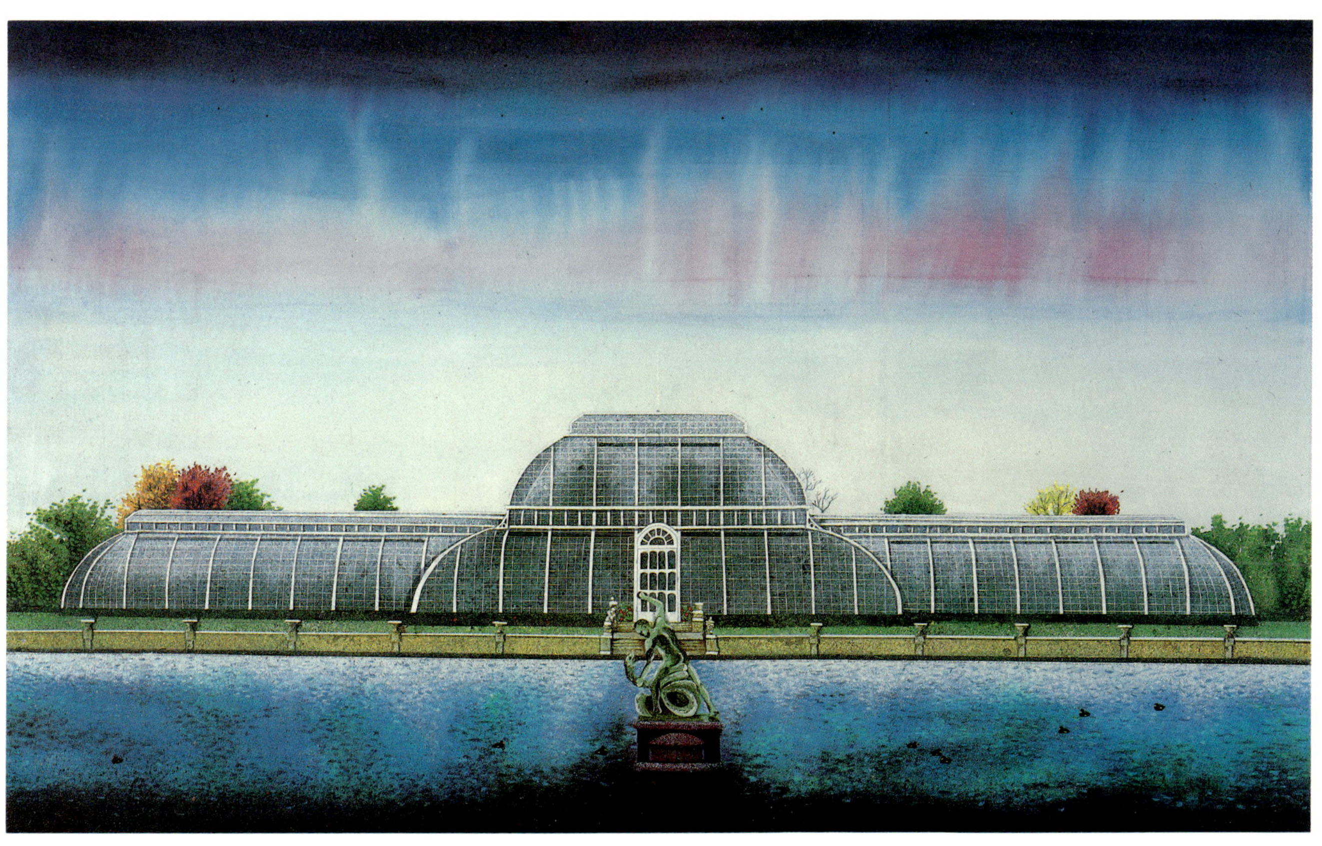

Plate 13 *Crystal Palace* 1979 (cat. 3)

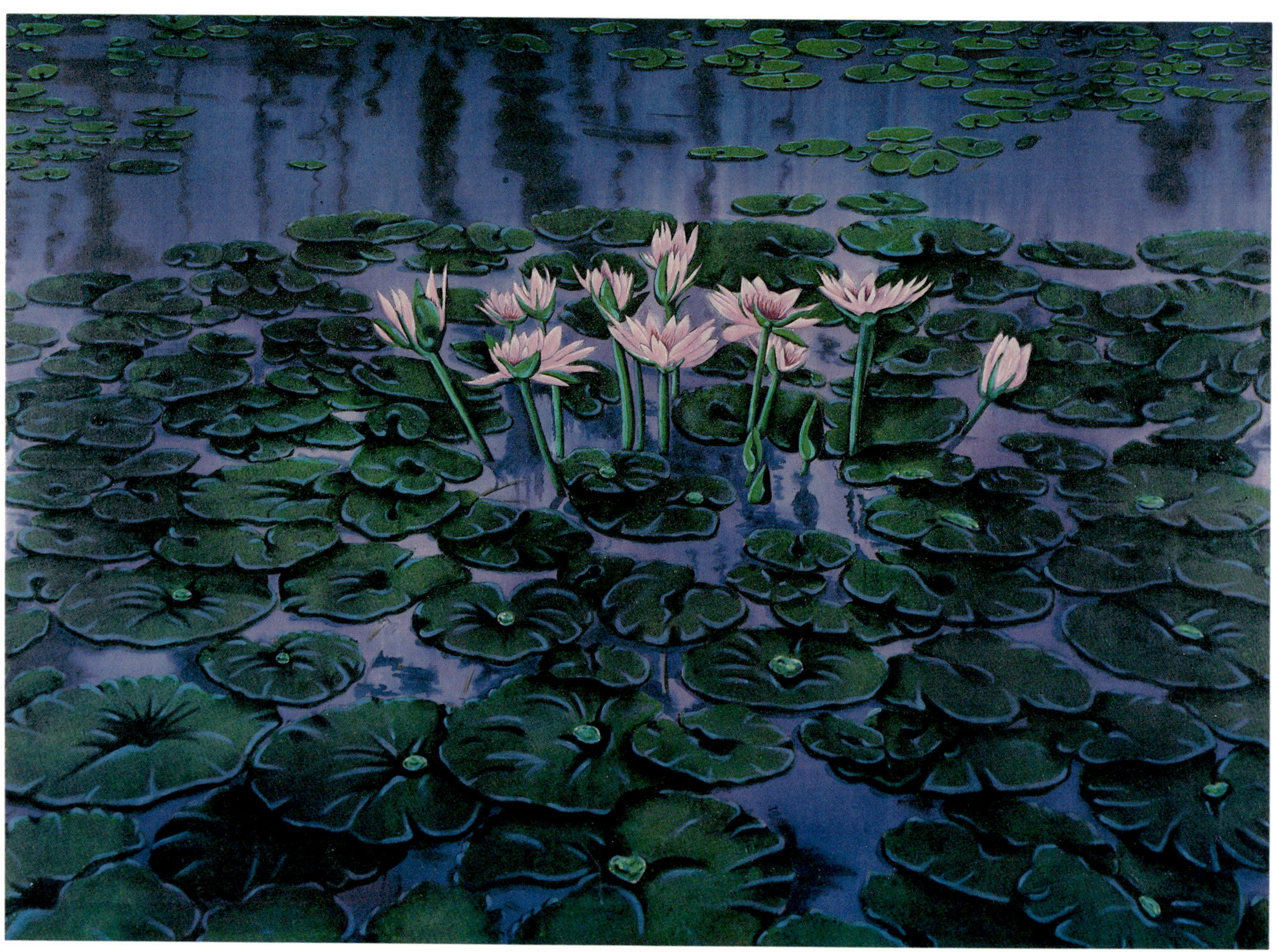

Plate 14 *Night Lilies* 1979 (cat. 5)

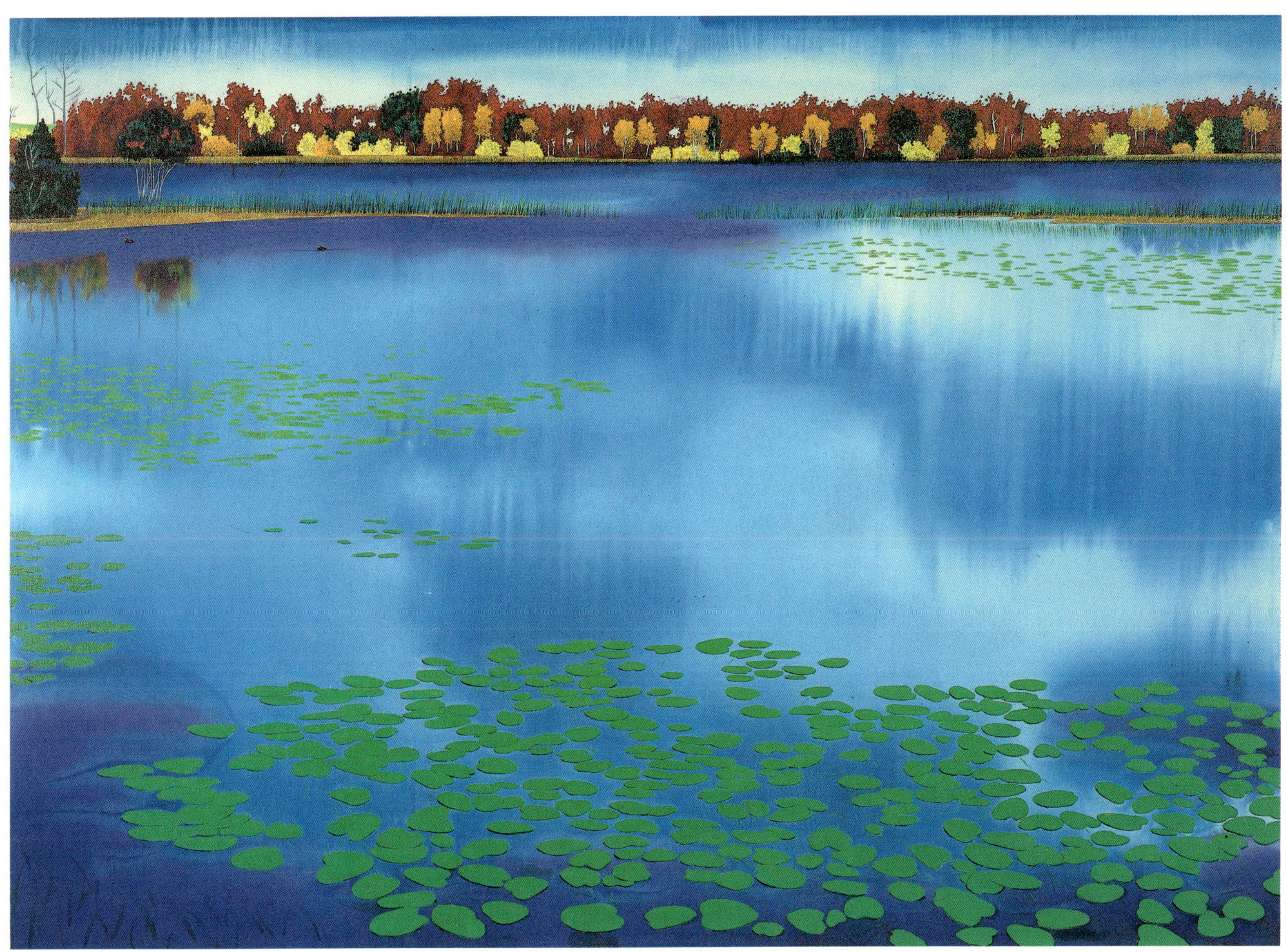

Plate 15 *Slough* 1979 (cat. 7)

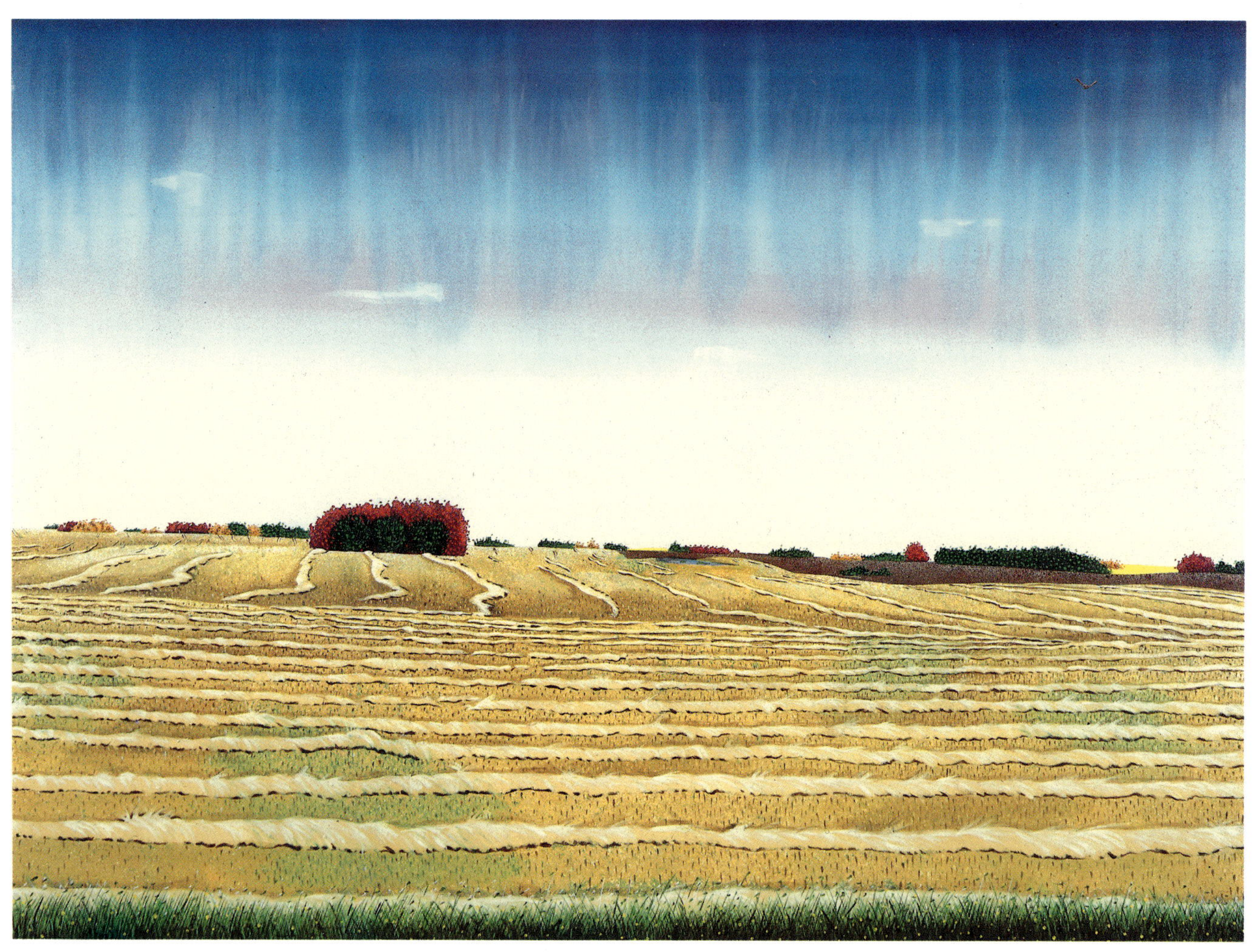

Plate 16 *Harvest Painting* 1979 (cat. 4)

a pleasure now available to an expanding middle class with the means and leisure time to indulge itself in diversions that can include, as is the case here, those of the senses. In *Slough,* the lilies sustain the theme of modernity in relation to landscape. Whatever fascination nature has had in western culture, it was only with the individualism and romanticism associated with the advent of modernity in the last century that landscape fully emerged as an acceptable and credible artistic genre. Moreover, however pastoral, it is difficult to contemplate a contemporary wheat field as abundant as the one pictured in *Harvest* apart from the modern technologies that inevitably support it.

In his consideration of modernity, Thauberger has concentrated on its legacy through an investigation of landscape, fantastic or visionary architecture, and domestic architecture. In this, working from a regional point of view has been crucial. One of the essential elements of Thauberger's art has been the identification of his community in mass cultural terms, a combination of popular memory, sentiment, fantasy and an often synthetic present comprising kitsch and the ever-present mass media — picture postcards, colour television, calendars, advertising, glossy magazines and the like. While sociologically this may be something of a distortion, as an abstraction it nonetheless rings true. Going back to the cooperative movement of the 1930s, Saskatchewan has been notably egalitarian and populist. As well, although today it is very much a middle-class, consumer and, with the decline of the family farm, an increasingly urban society, the province's way of life remains somewhat outside the contemporary urban mainstream. Examining modernity from the point of view of this particular society, its past and its present, its hopes and dreams, Thauberger has scrutinized the notions of progress and visions of arcadia at the heart of the modern experience as they are expressed through the representations, imagery, materials and values of mass culture. If this process has made a remarkable contribution to the definition of a given regional experience, in its involvement with mass cultural realities it has also pondered the fate of the modernist impulse in the contemporary middle-class society to which it gave impetus.

•

Landscape

Although Saskatchewan is not in any serious way cut-off from the world, a sense of isolation is a part of life in the province. Filtered through what might be thought of as a subjective, regional psychology of distance, far-off places can have an exotic allure. Thauberger has examined the play of this psychology through the depiction of landscape conceived not as tangible experience but as a state of mind. These landscapes have included such famous natural sites and wonders as Niagara Falls (pls. 22 and 23), Mount Rundle in Banff National Park (pl. 20) and Yellowstone National Park; generic landscapes based on popular landscape types, such as *Lake Reflecting Mountains,* 1982 (pl. 21), in which staples of the Canadian romantic vocabulary — a red canoe and mountain lake — are ostensibly manipulated to proper symbolic effect; and pre-historic landscapes, including

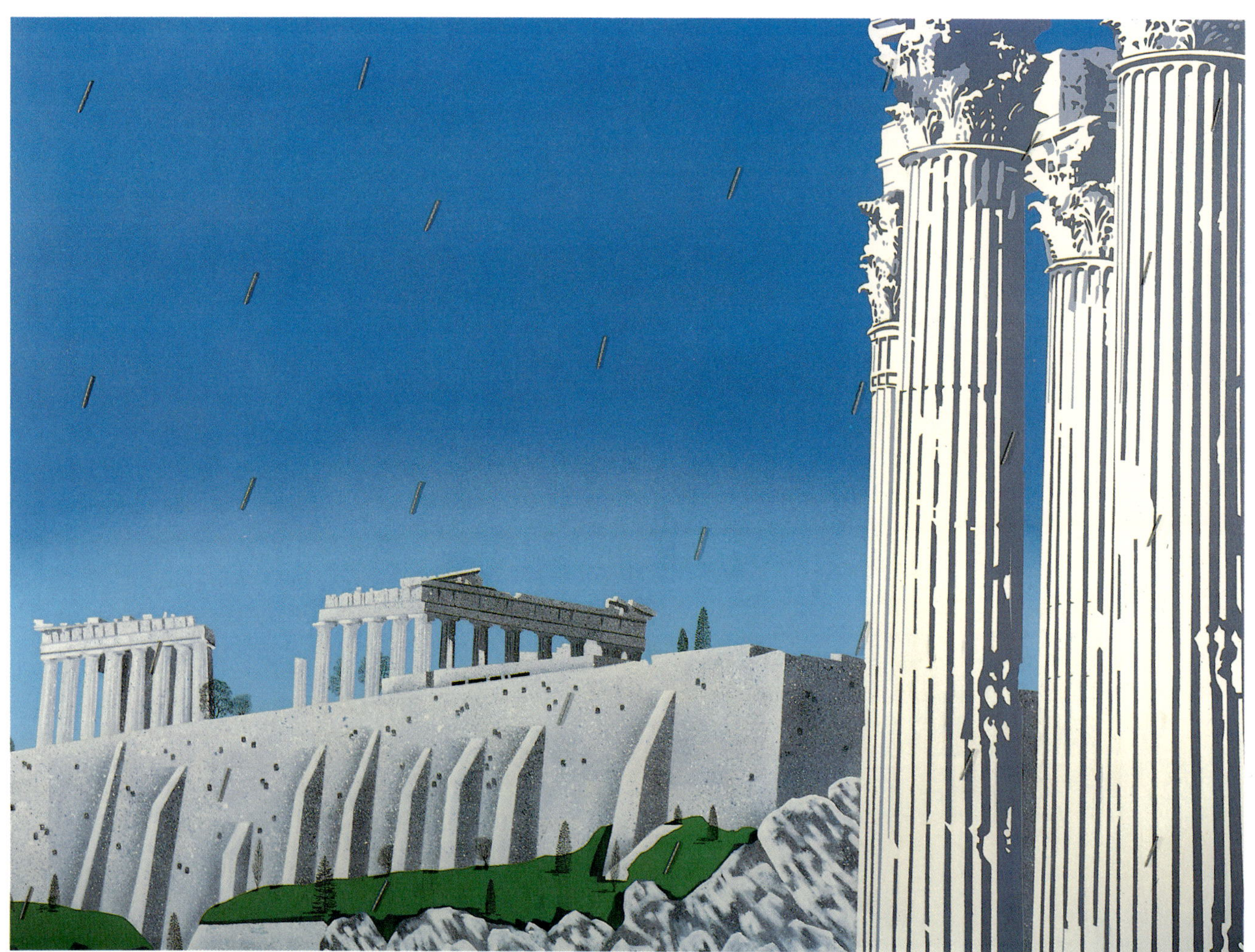

Plate 17 *Some Acid Rain* 1985 (cat. 29)

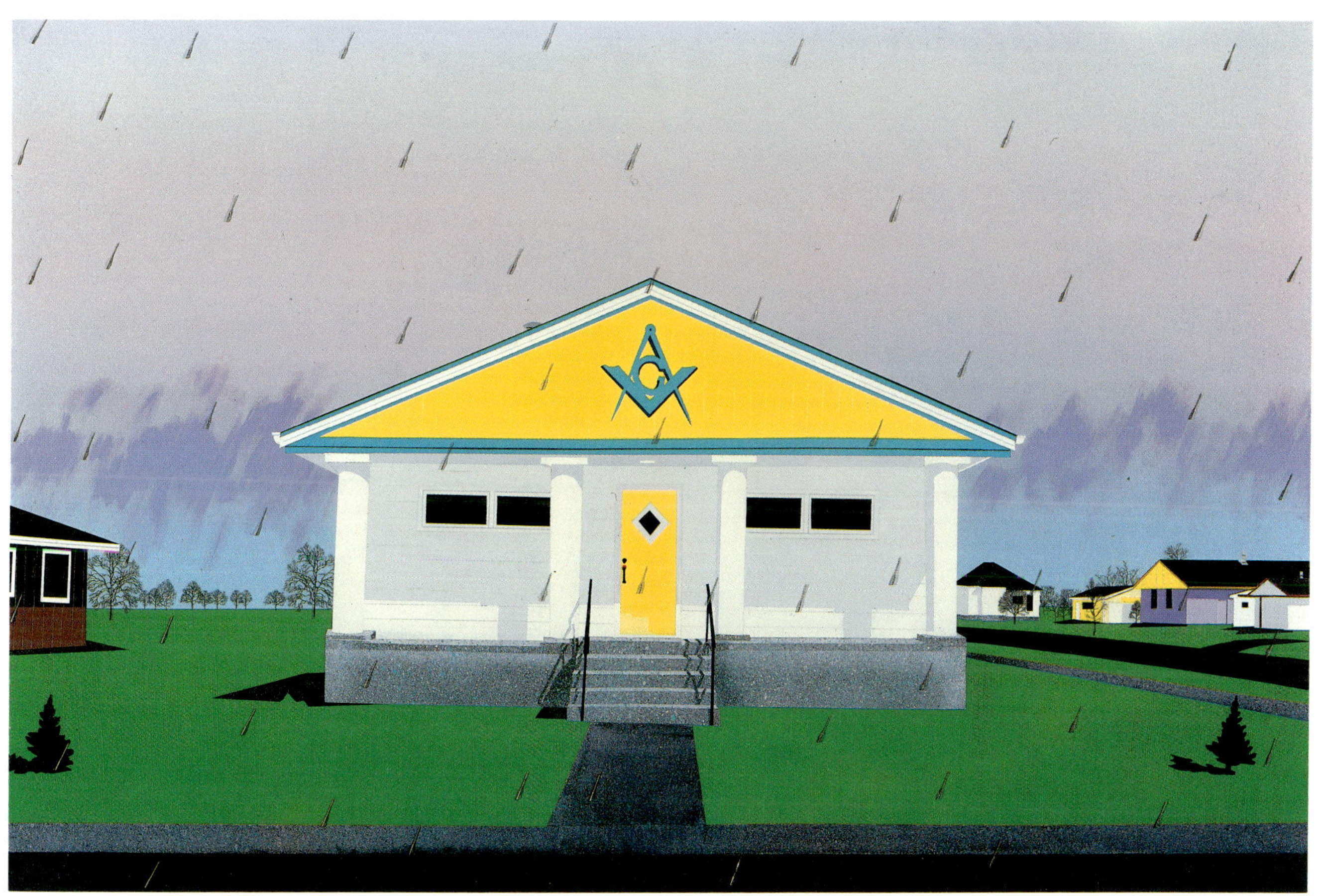

Plate 18 *Intermittent Shower* 1985 (cat. 26)

Machu Picchu (pl. 7) and the Easter Islands (pl. 24), in which the alluring mysteries of former cultures and civilizations provide a romanticized subject for highly dramatic images.

Thauberger's attitude towards these idealized images is one of affection. As far removed from reality as they may be, they are nevertheless an integral part of the social landscape with which he is concerned. They are about the desire that distance fuels and the fantasies that exist to satisfy them. As such, they have something significant, if ironic, to say about the experience of the prairies lacking in most work based on its actual observation. Yet another important aspect of these landscapes is that while Thauberger is mindful of their romantic and nostalgic appeal, they are not themselves romantic. Instead, depicted in terms of the rigid and artificial graphic conventions of the postcards and other commercial reproductions by which they are known and on which they are either directly or indirectly based, these works refer to the processes of idealization that foster and sustain such imagery. The inherently synthetic character of these images is difficult to ignore. Often there is a direct evocation of a media base, such as the inscription ''the rocky mtns'' on the painting of that name. Romantic illusion is challenged by the blatant artificiality and commercial nature of the materials and processes employed. Works are carefully composed and framed. In such paintings as *Seeing Double,* 1982 (pl. 19), there are mirror images that have an impressively crisp symmetry that may be suggested but is not realized in nature. Moreover, there is not even the hint of contact with nature. Reference is clearly, even explicitly confined to specific historical images or types of images that are of such currency that they are readily identifiable as clichés. In this context, it hardly matters that the scene in *Lake Reflecting Mountains,* so redolent of the image of Lake Louise nestled in the Canadian Rockies, is in fact a view of a famous lake in New Zealand, here copied from a magazine advertisement. Indeed, the point is largely that the two sites, as part of a common cultural language, are interchangeable.

Through the reflexiveness of these images, their romantic/anti-romantic dialectic, Thauberger not only underscores the role of culture in the formation and perception of reality, but representation itself is identified as fundamentally cultural. Rather than the product of individual insight, landscape is presented as a cultural phenomenon, a shared, collective vision. Comprised of a standard, and surprisingly limited, repertoire of images prominent within the history of romantic landscape painting, it is a vision that is constantly being reinforced through the recycling of these images, be it in art or, more pervasively, in various forms of mass media. In effect, the romantic landscape, essentially a phenomenon of nineteenth-century modernism, is understood in contemporary terms as a popular myth, a powerful, persistent, attractive but nonetheless imaginary construction. The issue is two-fold: the distinction between landscape as myth and the realities of what is very much a post-romantic age; the manner in which the present, subject to the attractions of such myths, accommodates the past to which they refer.

If the romantic landscape continues to be compelling, it is not difficult to understand. Reassuringly coherent, it connotes a harmonious relationship in which the natural world provides a vehicle for man's realization of meaning and truth. The image of Niagara Falls, for example, is associated historically with wonder, stability, progress, spirituality. The experience of nature as primal and elemental, another romantic theme alluded to by Thauberger, speaks of a kind of cleansing and the deferment to the imminent presence of a higher reality. In Canada, both in our literature and

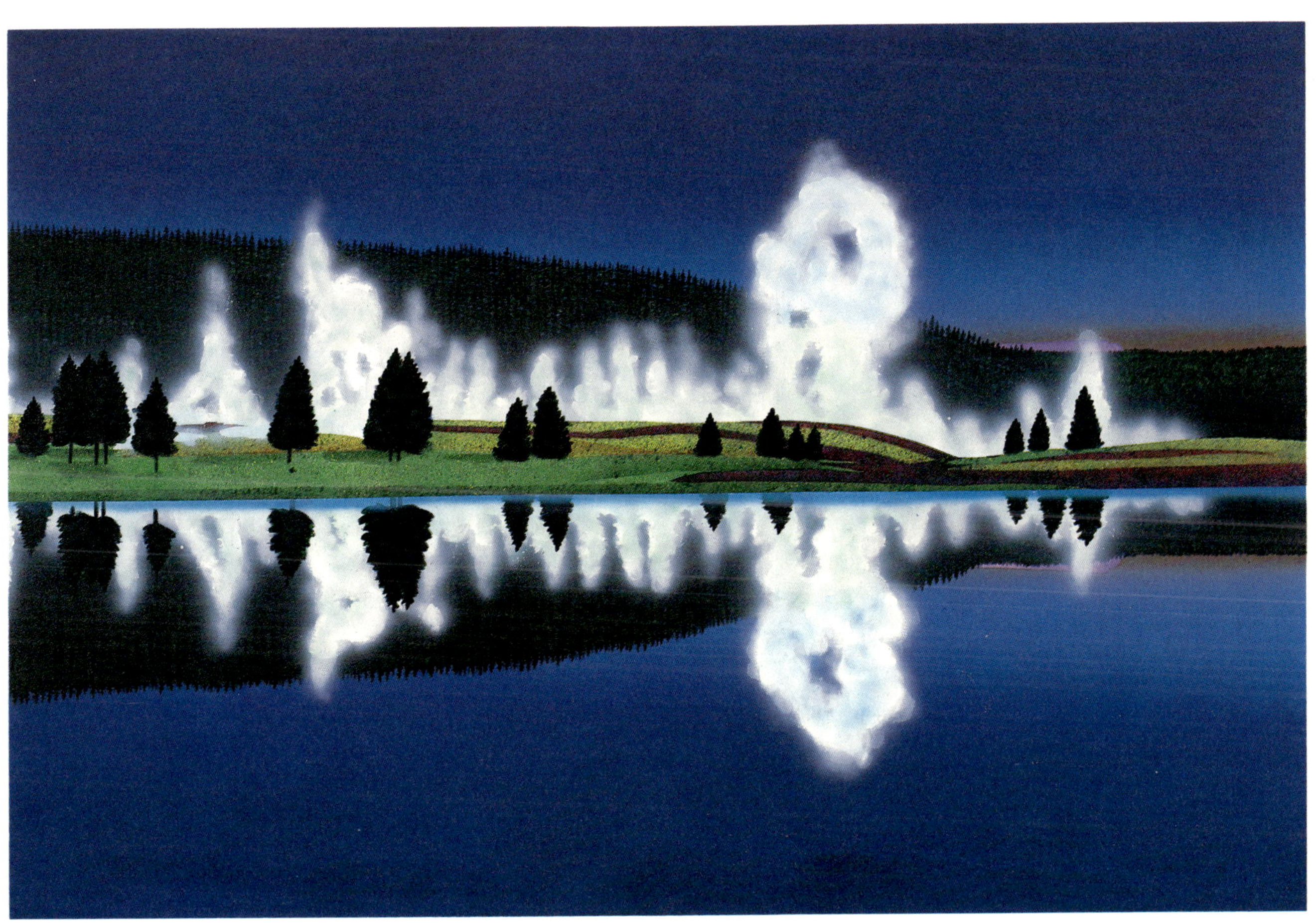

Plate 19 *Seeing Double* 1982 (cat. 18)

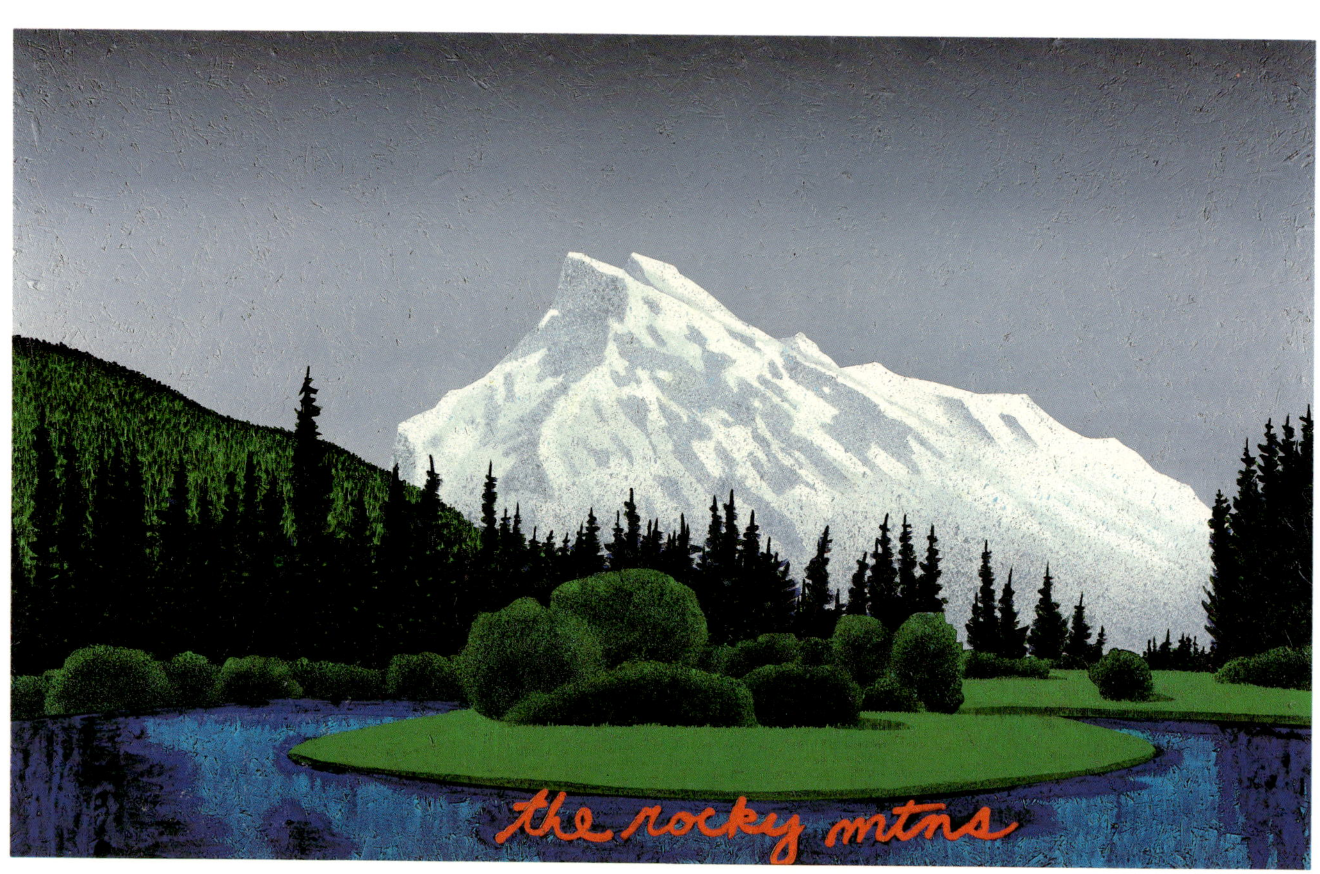

Plate 20 *the rocky mtns* 1982 (cat. 19)

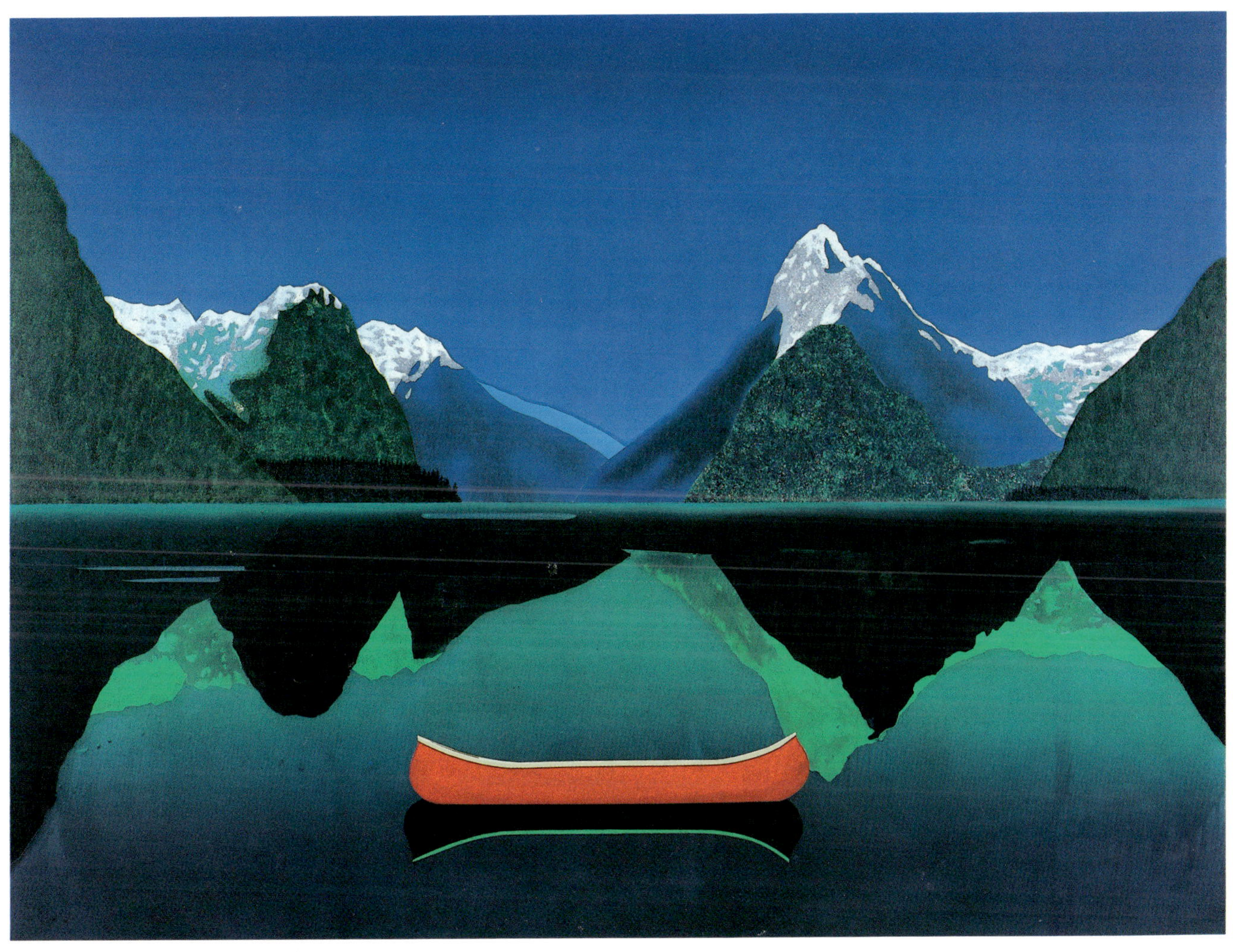

Plate 21 *Lake Reflecting Mountains* 1982 (cat. 17)

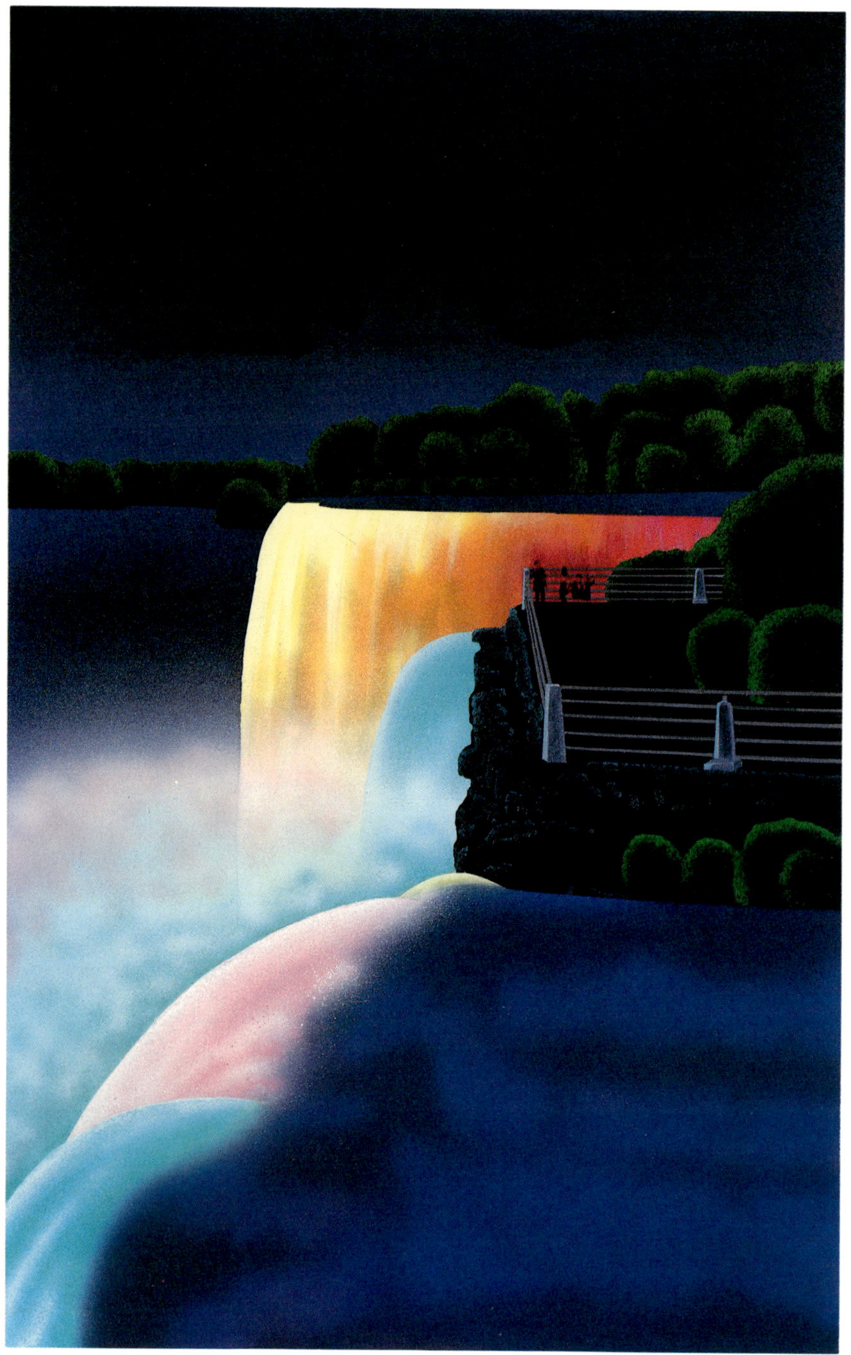

Plate 22 *Observation Point* 1983 (cat. 22)

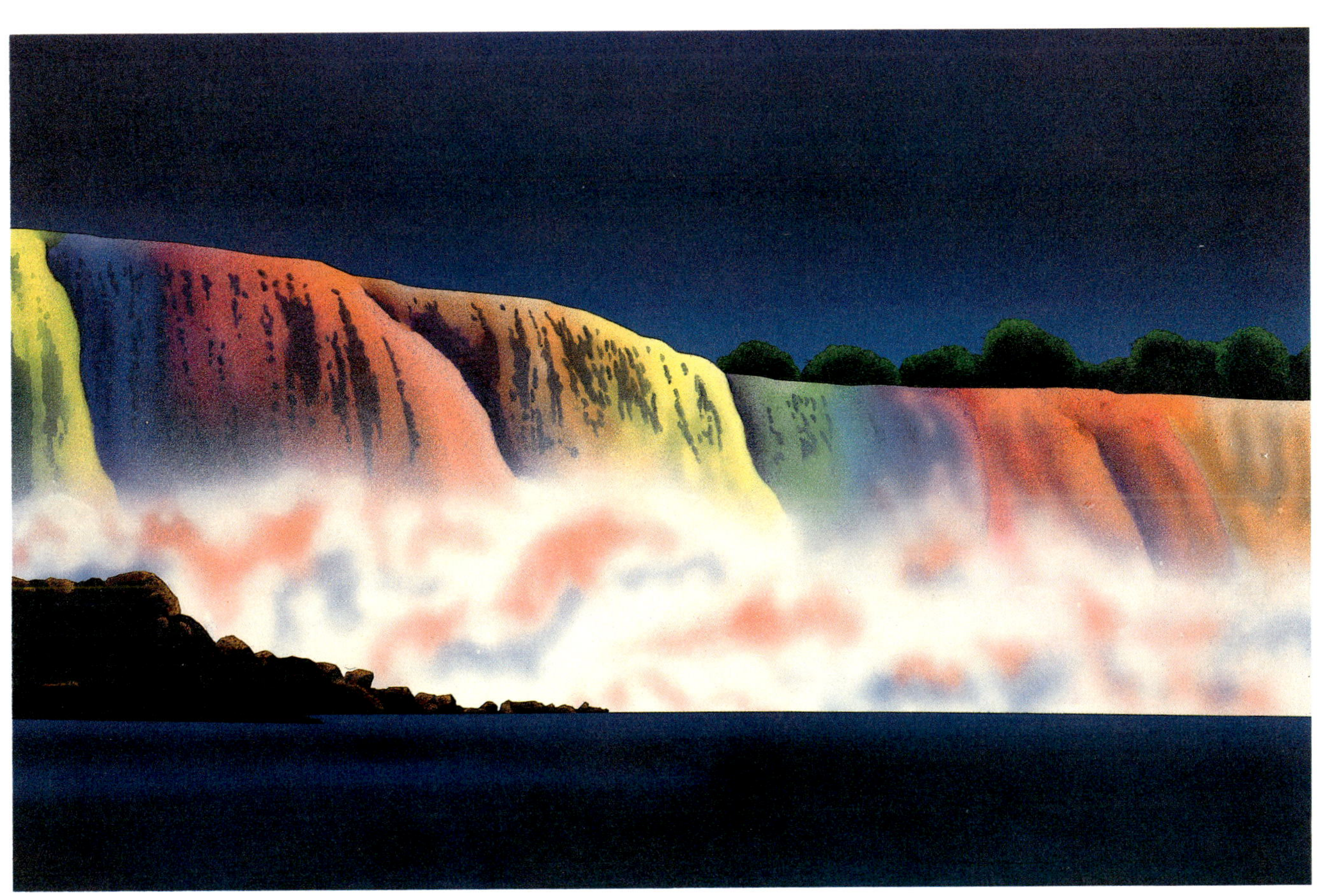

Plate 23 *Honeymoon Nights* 1983 (cat. 21)

visual arts, most evidently in the paintings of the Group of Seven, the wilderness has been seen, as it continues to be, as a framework within which identity can be established and defined. Yet if such images remain desirable, they are nonetheless problematic. In part this is because the conditions that gave rise to such representation of nature — a near obsessive fascination with it grounded in nature's presumed spiritual dimension; its purity, especially in relation to urban life; factual innocence — have long since passed. Indeed, rather than that reassuring sense of renewal for which it once stood, the natural world, exploited beyond reason, today suggests only fragility. If it retains a role as a symbol, then it is as one of extreme vulnerability if not despair.

In turning in these landscapes to models drawn from the past, Thauberger is not seeking either their conventional meanings or solace. The loss of our traditional empathy with nature is not mourned, nor is an attempt made to breathe new life into that relationship. The intent, rather, is to maintain a more meaningful relationship with a past landscape represents, one which provides the present with a context rather than an ideal. In this sense, Thauberger's repetition of these images might be understood as positive acts of memory. By presenting them in terms of their representations, these images make contact with history rather than repeat it.[15] The same nostalgic desire that continues to make the sites he depicts such popular tourist meccas is pervasive but, within the controlled terms of this methodology, it does not operate as an expression of wish fulfillment. Great admiration and awareness of past efforts is suggested, yet a critically clear distinction is drawn. In *the rocky mtns,* Thauberger has referred through his image of Mount Rundle to Cézanne's famous versions of Mont Sainte-Victoire. Here, however, the master's beautiful brushwork has been simulated through the substitution of an inexpensive chipboard for the traditional stretched canvas surface. And, whereas Cézanne is understood to have struggled heroically with the representation of the mountain, Thauberger has simply run up a good postcard view, lightened all that much more by the bright red text planted in the lower foreground. In a related vein, Niagara Falls may be sublime, but its sublimity in Thauberger's paintings relates more to the honeymoon suite than matters of the spirit. And, despite its canoe and majestic lake, as a romantic image, *Lake Reflecting Mountains* is too dramatic, owes too great a debt to photo-mechanical reproduction, to truly engage the sentiments with which this iconography is associated.

In a different critical perspective, the proliferation of forms of popular expression, the postcard and other such images of which Thauberger is so fond, might be seen to disturb, manipulate or, as kitsch, to trivialize nature. Here, however, they operate as an emotionally rich link to the modernist values of a more optimistic and perhaps more innocent age, a romantic streak that is nonetheless understood as still deeply implicated in the attitudes of the present. Distanced and vigilant with respect to past traditions, these landscapes are highly sensitive to present realities.

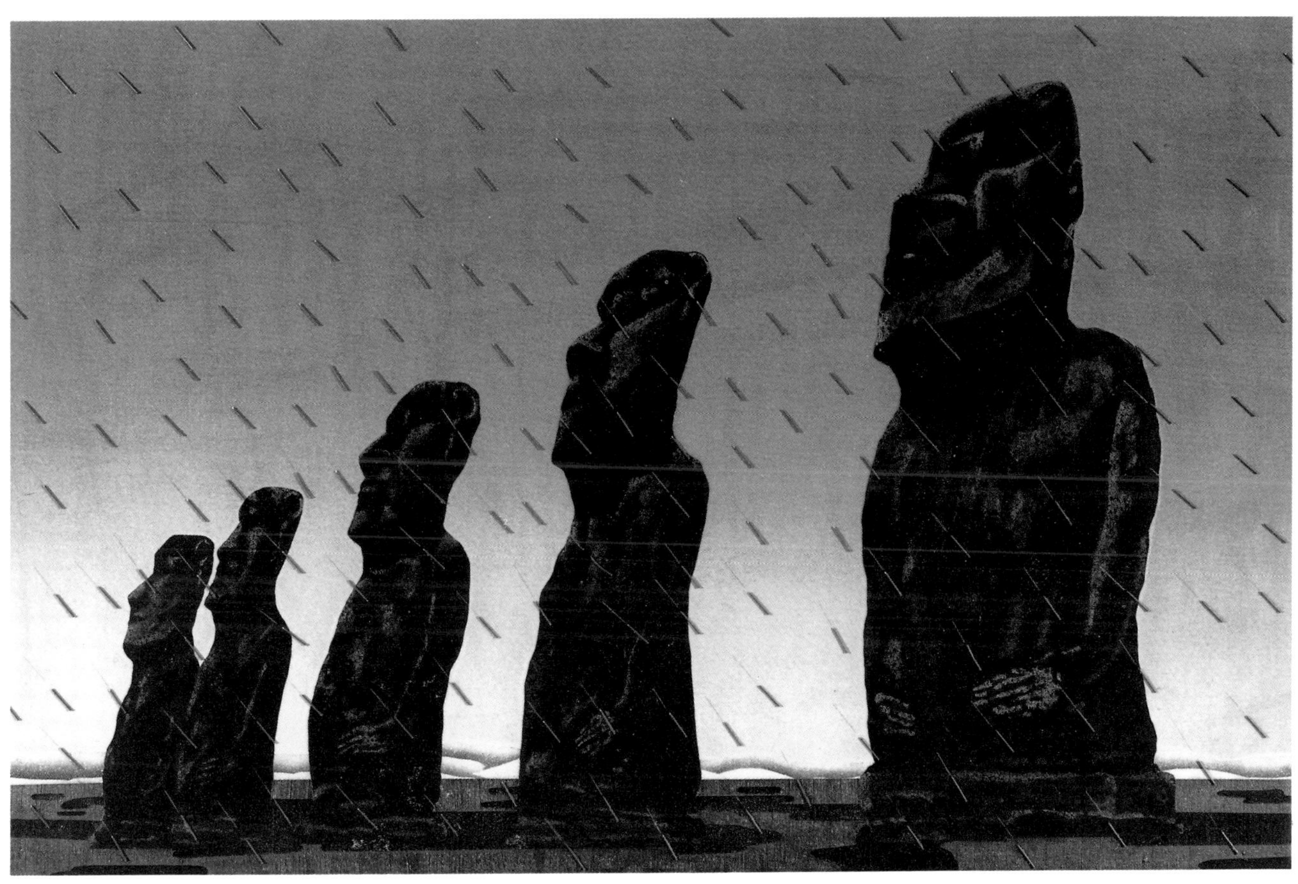

Plate 24 *Driving Rain* 1984 (cat. 23)

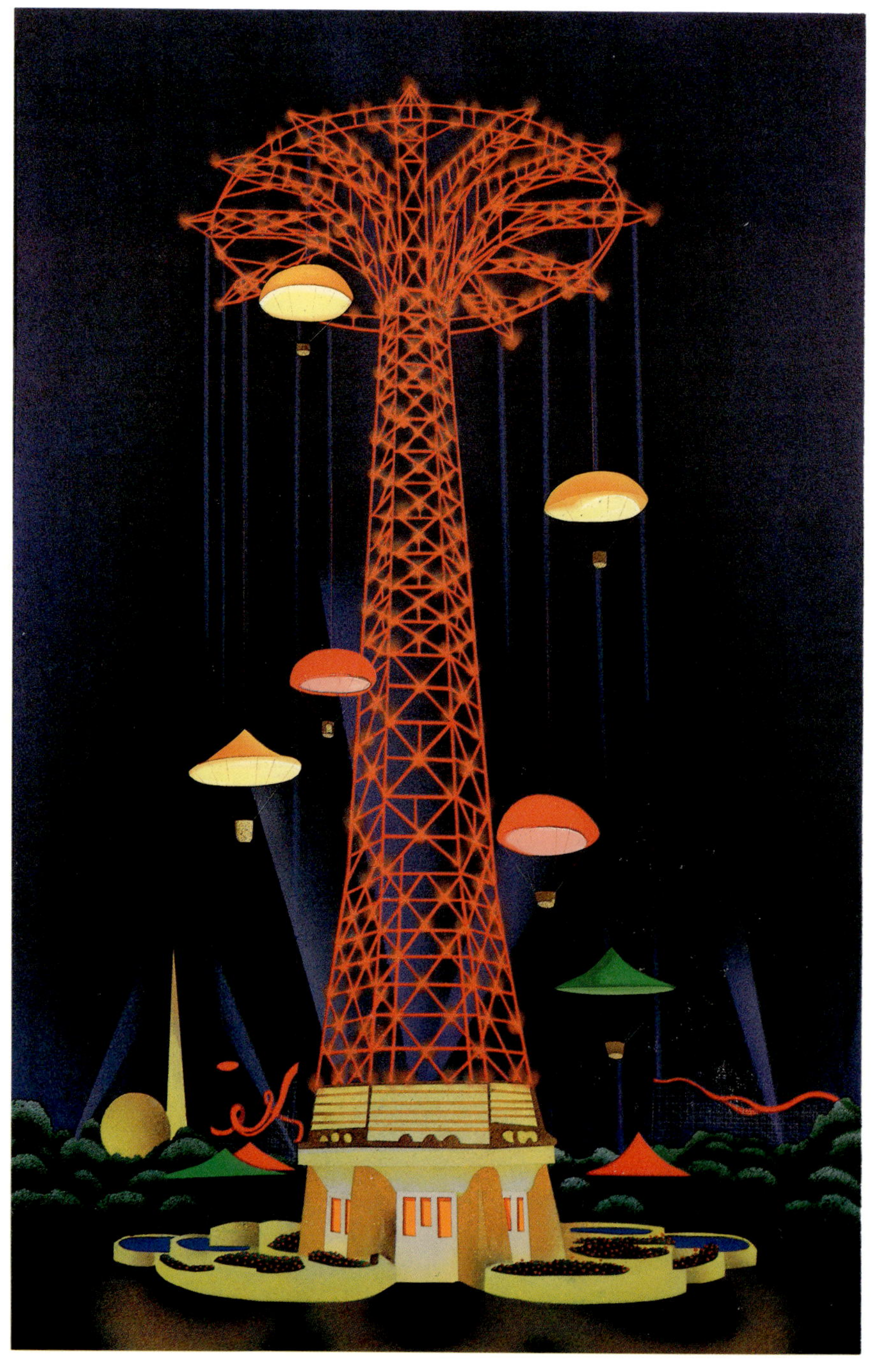

Plate 25 *Parachute Jump* 1986 (cat. 32)

Fantastic Architecture

The Jump was sponsored by the Life Savers candy company. I looked up. Big Life Savers of every color were affixed to the metal lacework of the parachute tower. That was consoling. . .This was not a true parachute jump, but more like the feeling a fireman would have sliding down a brass pole. That was fine with me. There was a lurch, and we began our rise. My heart beat furiously. I went rigid and held my breath. Up we rose, higher and higher, I could see the whole Fair dropping away under us, the shining white Trylon and Perisphere were bathed now in pale blue light. I saw the Lagoon of Nations, its fountains lit in many colors. I saw the Aquacade. I heard music from a dozen directions, and then, as we rose the breeze added itself to the music like a string section, but in a mocking way of fluctuating sound, as if we would never stop rising from the earth and were bound now for another realm of fierce winds and darkness, a sky life, and we would be blown about in it forever.
E. L. Doctorow
World's Fair[16]

The young protagonist's ride on the Parachute Jump is a climactic moment in E. L. Doctorow's 1985 novel in which hopes for a bright, shining future are bound up with the visions of the 1939/40 New York World's Fair. Yet the ride, like the fair, is something of an anti-climax. Doctorow views the Parachute Jump with ambivalence. It is, after all, a romance manufactured to promote candy. And, however dynamic the appearance of its towering, vertical form, the thing itself is rather rickety. The ride, it turns out, is not really like floating on air. Moreover, while something like a transcendent experience does occur, it doesn't take much to bring the whole experience back down to earth. ''I swore that if I came out of this alive, never again would I go up in such a contraption.''[17]

On the surface at least, Thauberger's image of the Parachute Jump (pl. 25) and other architectural extravaganzas of the 1939/40 World's Fair (pls. 26–28) is rather less equivocal than Doctorow's. In these paintings, the fair is presented as a glowing vision of utopian wonder and splendor. Like the Crystal Palace, these structures, streamlined and geometric, would seem to embody the hopes and faith vested in modern technology's capacity to positively transform life through a seemingly transcendental rationality. There are, however, difficulties here. In the almost half-century since the fair, during which it has remained a powerful modernist statement, the shallowness of this vision has become only too clear. As Arthur C. Clarke has said, ''The future isn't what it used to be.'' Technology has not only not always delivered, but it has proven to be socially alienating and, in many cases, a positive threat to existence itself. These questions are further compounded by Thauberger's point of departure for these paintings and their unstated subject, the 1986 Vancouver World's Fair. In failing to capture the public imagination in any significant way, the Vancouver Fair demonstrated, if nothing else, the degree to which the tradition of world expositions as all-encompassing visions of progress have lost relevance. In addition, like his landscapes, these paintings are based on existing popular imagery, in this instance vintage postcards. Presenting the fair as it chose to see itself, these works are about images, image-making and the wizardry, magic and power of illusion. Indeed, as the following passage from the 1939 fair guide book suggests, for some fair planners at least, illusion would seem to have taken precedence over social change:

> Visible for miles around, a flood of multi-colored light drenches the sky above the glowing spectacle that is the Fair at night. Light, fire, color, water, and sound have been ingeniously and subtly blended to create a dazzling scene that embraces every band of the spectrum...The

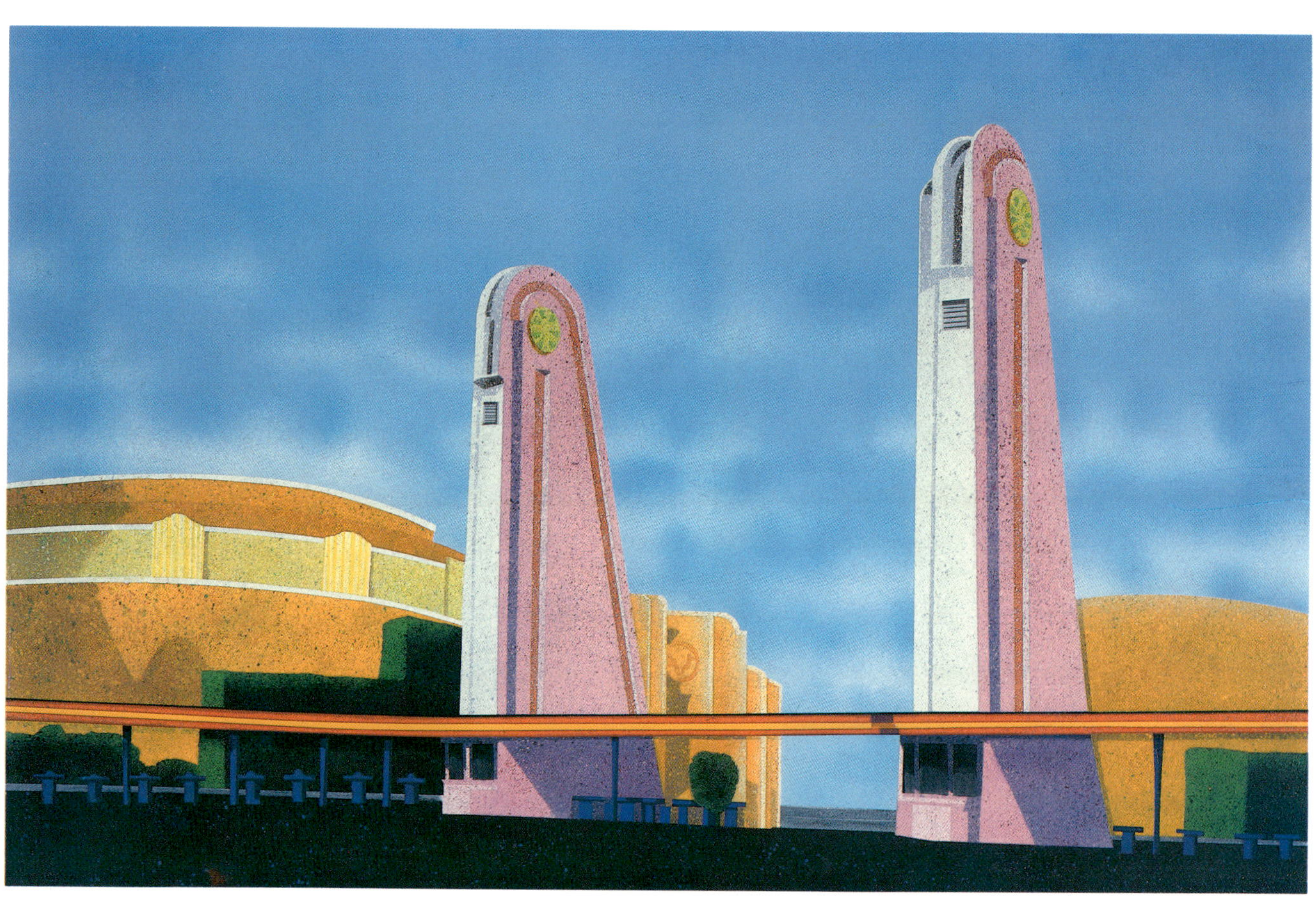

Plate 26 *Corona North* 1986 (cat. 30)

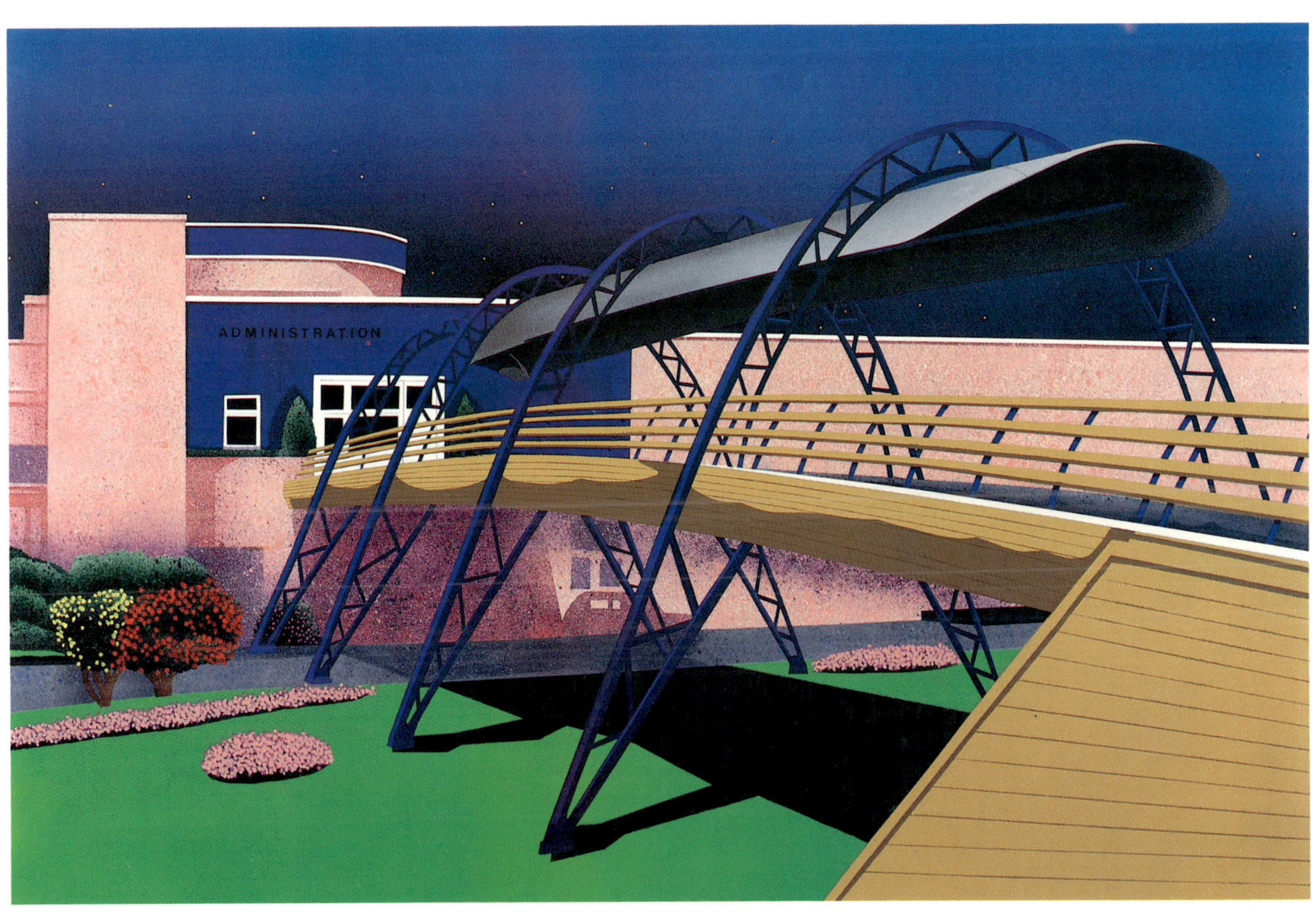

Plate. 27 *Space Bridge* 1986 (cat. 33)

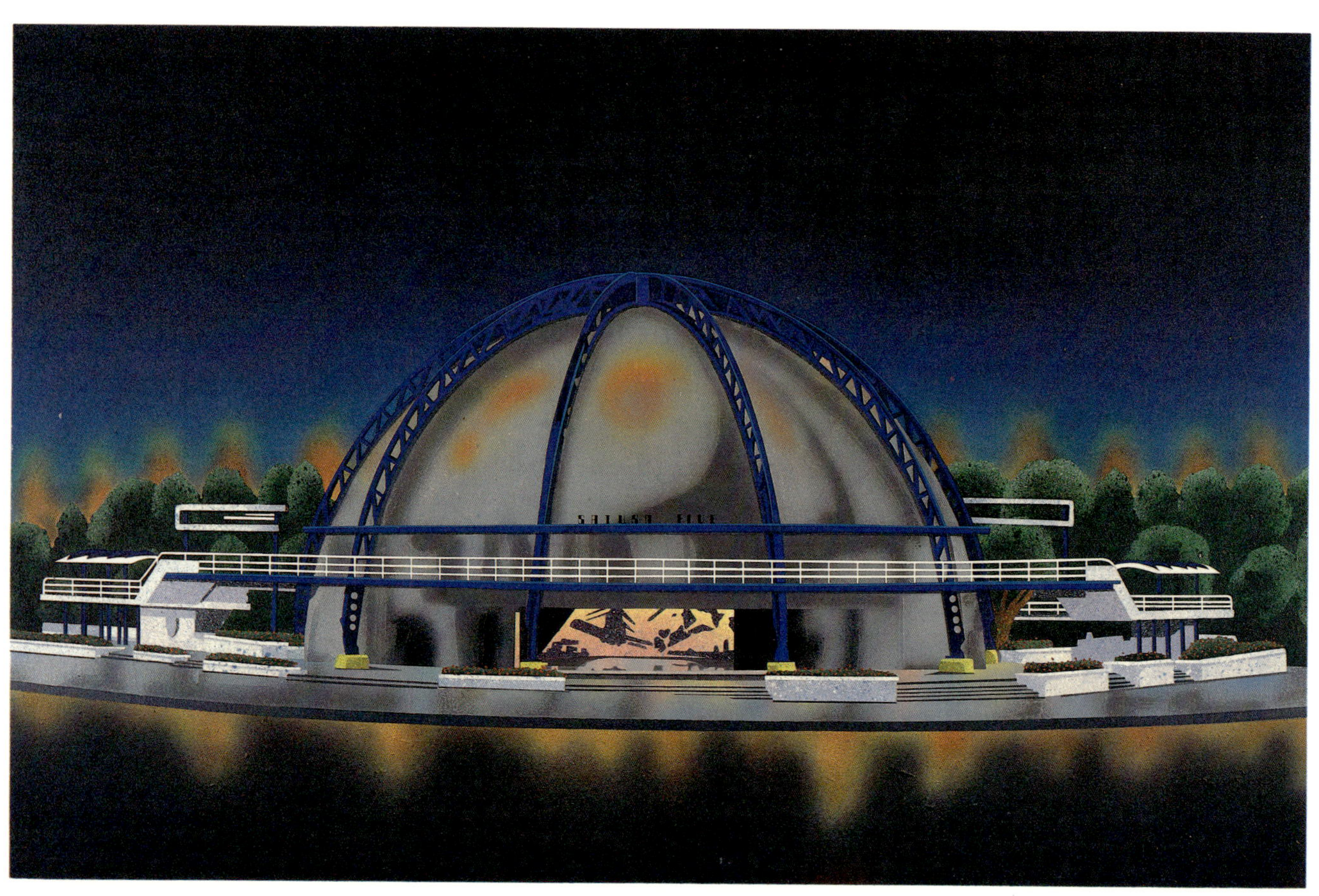

Plate 28 *Steel Pavilion* 1986 (cat. 35)

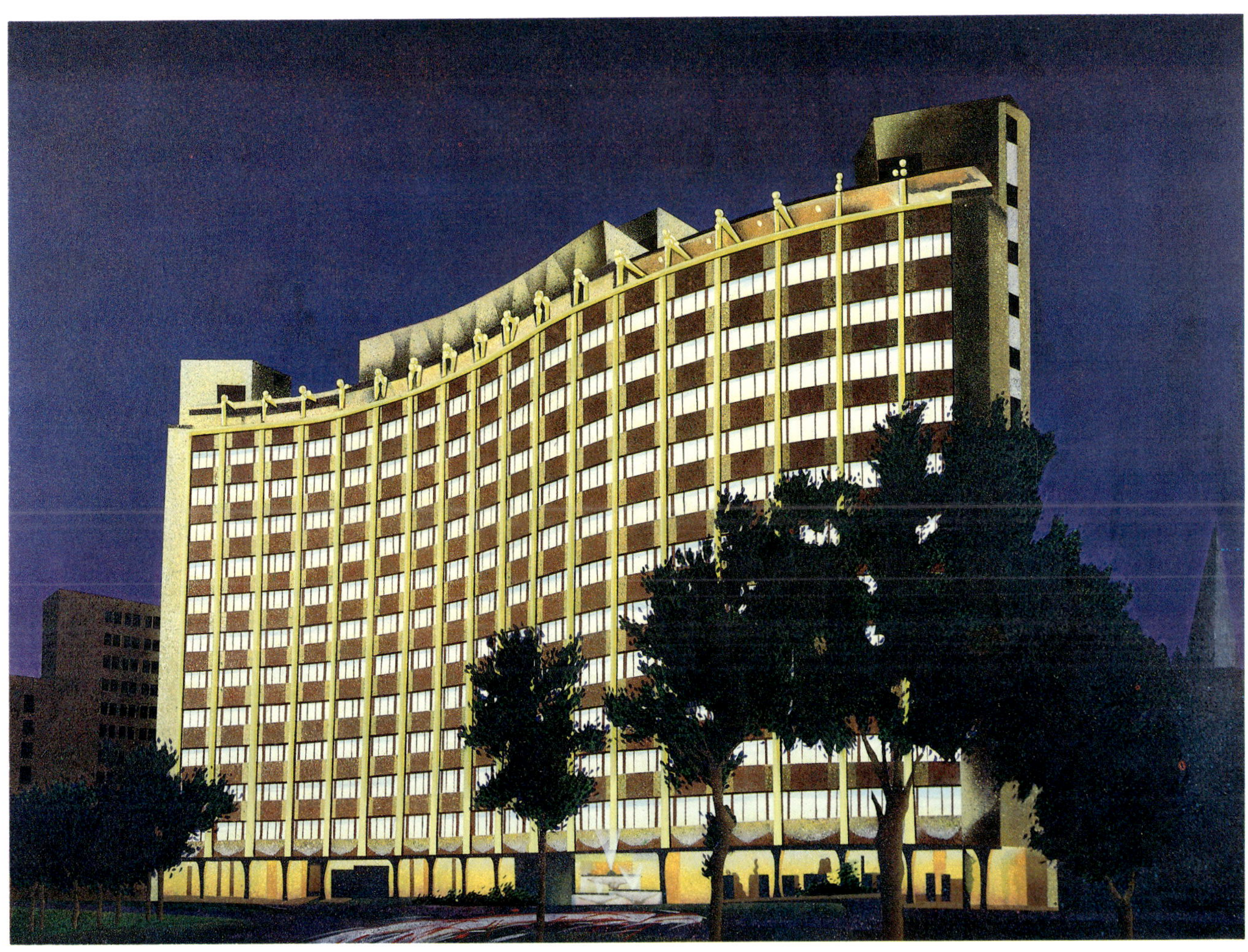

Plate 29 *All That Glitter* 1980 (cat. 8)

city of magic, it might well be called, an enchanting vision hinting at the future in artificial illumination.[18]

Despite his recognition that the visionary remains a fantasy rather than a reality, Thauberger, like Doctorow, is only too aware of the importance of these past projections. Like his landscapes, these structures are significant as points of reference for the present. In this, there is a significant irony, for it is the symbols of an attitude that spurned the past that are called upon to provide perspective on a present that can be seen, in some sense at least, as the rather fragile product of that attitude. Yet it is through such contradictions and ironies that these works operate. The fair was a dream of the future but, as its critics have pointed out, that future was short-sighted, an unrestrained consumer culture driven largely by big business and industry. Discussing Democracity, the fair's theme pavilion, one critic has written that it was "curiously static, sterile, and unreal..." Its "vision of the future was a planner's version of regional urban sprawl, a vast Utopian stage set. The vaguely humanitarian ideals that inspired it were...psychologically and practically untenable...as the history of the American suburb has amply demonstrated in the half-century since. It seemed to deny the existence of the poor, the incompetent, and the racially and ethnically dispossessed . . . "[19]

Through their remove, Thauberger's heightened images of the fair broach these well-taken points. The totalitarian overtones of the fair's architecture and display techniques are apparent. Yet these paintings also point to something else. This is not so much those humanitarian ideals or naive, and admittedly constricted, notions of democracy as it is some sense of the fair as a popular event. Seeing through its ideological hype, the evident spectacle, its obvious disappointments, the fair is also presented in terms of the pleasure it was capable of providing. Despite its controversial status, to this day the 1939/40 World's Fair is remembered with affection as an event of great vitality to which people were strongly responsive at the end of an extended and trying period of deprivation. Not coincidentally, the Crystal Palace, re-erected on a new site several years after the Great International Exposition, was itself immensely popular with the London public which, unlike the structure's critics, found in the building something both exciting and moving.[20] It's not difficult to understand. However unreal, dream and fantasy are also a part of life.

In part, this response to the fair's architecture is tied to the exoticism of its often bizarre and ingratiating forms. Rather than the classic, international style box, many of the fair's buildings were strongly sculptural and pictorial. Their geometry was a rounded deco. They were ornamented, coloured and imaginatively lit. If they could be seen as imposing, they were also pleasing, dramatic, fanciful.[21] With respect to Thauberger's work, their significance is amplified by reference to his painting *All That Glitter,* 1980 (pl. 29). The office tower in *All That Glitter* is, by any account, an eccentric modern building. It is the work of a local Regina architect whose indebtedness to the elegant, antirational designs of the Spanish architect Antonio Gaudi is evident in the building's signal feature, a laterally extended, undulating facade.[22] The building could be a mere curiosity but isn't. The reason relates both to its scale, which, while grand, is not inhuman, and to the warmth and attractiveness of a form that, like the fair pavilions, far exceeds its function. In a city the size of Regina, the building not only works but it can perhaps be seen to symbolize a modernism that, in a capacity to adapt itself to circumstance and place, embodies the desire to please and refresh life that so vividly animates the fair architecture Thauberger has found so intriguing.

Domestic Architecture

If landscape and fantastic architecture represent a paradoxical desire for transcendence of the every-day conditions of modernist life, the idea of the suburban, single-family home, an amalgam of agrarian and urban impulses, represents modernist hope in terms of what, in North America at least, has been its perhaps most concrete and palpable experience. The expression of a deeply felt cultural outlook that goes back to the flight of the eighteenth-century English merchant class from the inner city, the surburban home embodies a desire for a life of privacy, independence and property in the context of the nuclear family.[23] For the past ten years, Thauberger has surveyed this ideal in his immediate environment through the depiction of domestic architecture. On the one hand, these paintings, with their sensitivity to the characteristics and particular nuances of various period styles, are simply a form of architectural history. But they are also social and cultural history. From modest, older bungalows to the contemporary suburban split-level with its two-car garage, these works chronicle the evolution of the domestic residence as a sign of the middle-class dream of a better life through the potential for social migration. Keying the point of view here, Thauberger's titles are especially significant: *Little Dream Home* (fig. 13), *Dream Home (Ethnic Version)* (pl. 30), *Starter* (pl. 31), *Doll's House* (cover), *Late Bloomer* (pl. 32), *Double Happiness* (pl. 33), *Pride of Ownership* (pl. 34).

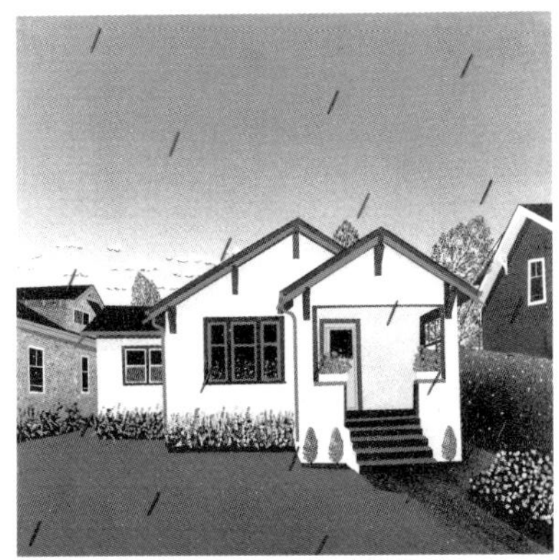

Fig. 13 *Little Dream Home* 1985 (cat. 27)

Although they are based on actual buildings, these paintings are no more realistic or natural-istic than Thauberger's other works. With their neatly manicured lawns, flowers, gardens, decorative coloration, prim condition and straight-on views, all of these homes may not exactly be material for *Better Homes and Gardens,* but they are nonetheless attractive. The image that is projected is one of comfort, well-being and happiness, of subjectivity realized through a harmonious balance of arcadian vision and a due consideration of the practicalities that go with material prosperity. The difficulty with such an image, of course, is that it is an image. The modern suburb has long been seen as a social failure, whether it is as the haven for social and economic privilege it represented in the earlier, more strictly bourgeois concept of the garden city, or, its more recent mass reality, characterized by the seemingly unchecked development of architectural boxes, itself tied to the mushrooming of a kind of bland, numbing social conformity. The psychological price of such dream homes has also been recognized. There is more than a little irony, for example, in Thauberger's charming and distinctive *Doll's House,* a painting which takes its title from the name of a well-known Regina architectural landmark on which it is based. In his 1898 suburban novel, *A Man From the North,* it was the image of the doll's house that Arnold Bennett used to represent the decline of optimism for his aspiring writer-hero. "He knew well that he would make no further attempt to write. Laura...worshipped him, he felt sure, and at times he had a great tenderness for her; but it would be impossible to write in the suburban doll's house which was to be theirs'."[24] As a contemporary critic has noted, "No late nineteenth-century reader who knew their Ibsen would be likely to be unmoved by this particular hint at the stifling life in store...for both partners."[25] To this image might be added a more current one, the spiritless environment of the consumer society.

The limitations of the idea of the dream home and the values that support it are most strong-ly suggested in Thauberger's paintings of contemporary houses. Despite its striking presence,

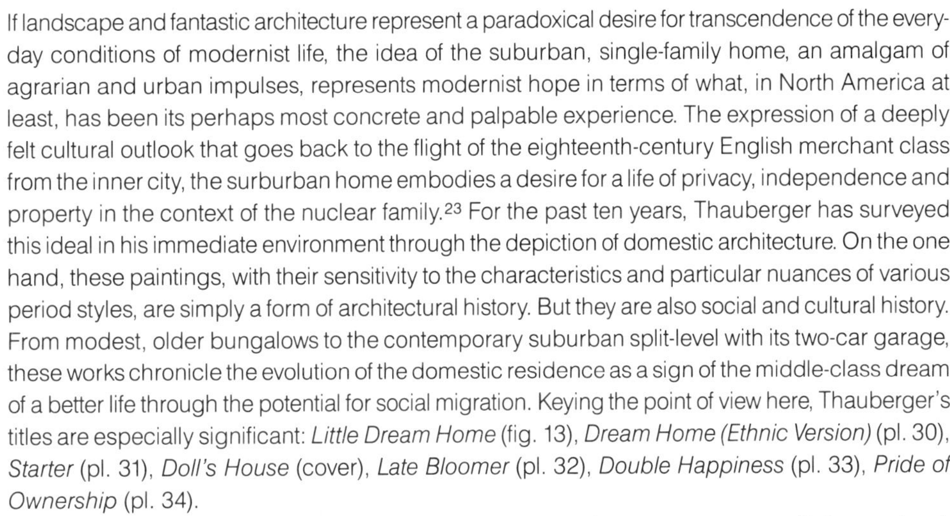

Pride of Ownership is set against a sky of such lurid electricity it is disturbing. Composed of two variations on the standard cube, the house can be seen to suggest the chilly implications of Le Corbusier's modernist ideal of the home as "a machine to live in." Similarly, the rationalized design of the modern duplex in *Double Happiness* may be highly efficient, but the painting does not necessarily suggest that happiness is its true subject. Nonetheless, there are hedges against this form of architectural order. In the case of *Pride of Ownership,* it is the colours of the house. Adventurous or garish, depending on how one chooses to see them, they stand in striking contradiction to the pristine refinement associated with Le Corbusier's vision. In *Double Happiness* it is the front walk which, divided in front of the house by a flower bed and standing evergreen, takes on the air, however humble, of a processional. If these houses express themselves almost against their architecture, Thauberger's bungalows suggest an important point of reference. Presented as contemporary rather than historic views, these houses represent not simply a nostalgia for the past but an affection based on a recognition that the ornamentation and decoration, the sense of warmth and comfort associated with the past are valued and important.

Discussing this feeling for the past in his study of the home, the architectural historian Witold Rybczynski asks: "Is it simply a curious anachronism, this desire for tradition, or is it a reflection of a deeper dissatisfaction with the surroundings that our modern world has created? What are we missing that we look so hard for in the past?"[26] What is missing, it would appear, is what Thauberger is addressing in these paintings, the sense of social coherence that both underlies the notion of home and spurs dissatisfaction with the modern world. In a sense, that coherence would not seem to be out of line with the historic suburban vision. Yet, contemporary reality has little chance against what remains an eighteenth-century ideal. Instead, working from a strongly articulated regionalist perspective, Thauberger has located this community at the point where modernist ideals meet the diffuse patterns and intensified experience of the contemporary world. The society he presents is pluralist, middle-of-the-road and, significantly, one that finds meaning through engagement with both the dynamics of a complex and changing environment and the past. Though it harbours utopian dreams, it is not presented as a utopian society or a model for such. It is, rather, a place where a home is conceived and made through the acceptance and refusal referred to by Mandel, "a moral act, an awareness of integrity, an affirmation."[27]

1. Eli Mandel, "Culture and Literacy: Contemporary Canadian Writing," The Mary Donaldson Memorial Lecture, 1979, Saskatchewan Library Association; reprinted as "Academic and Popular," in Eli Mandel, *The Family Romance* (Winnipeg: Turnstone Press, 1986), pp. 43–57.

2. For a related statement concerning the effacement of the boundaries between high art and mass culture see Fredric Jameson, "Postmodernism and Consumer Society," in *The Anti-Esthetic: Essays in Postmodern Culture,* edited by Hal Foster (Port Townsend, Washington: Bay Press, 1983), p. 112.

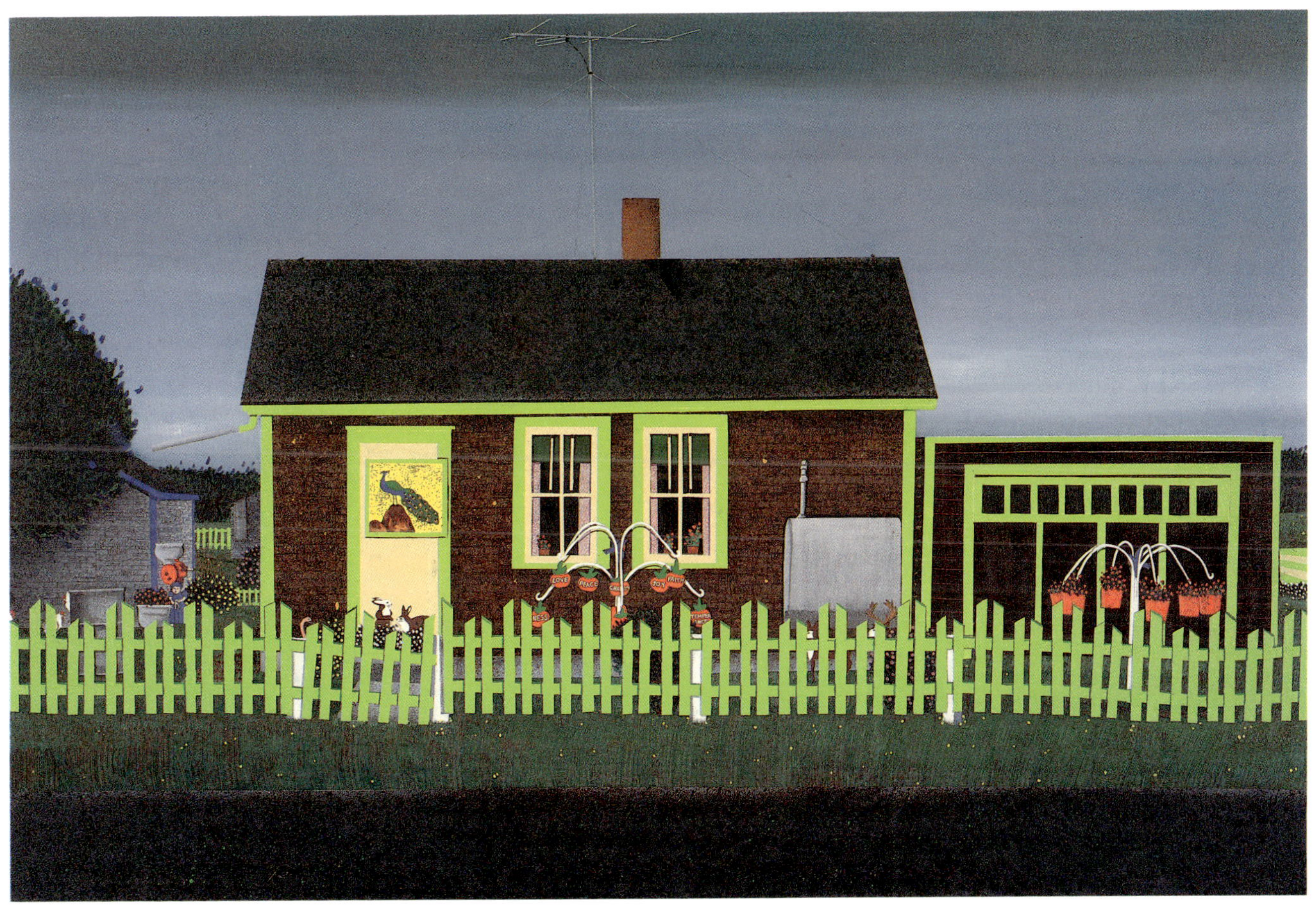

Plate 30 *Dream Home (Ethnic Version)* 1980 (cat. 11)

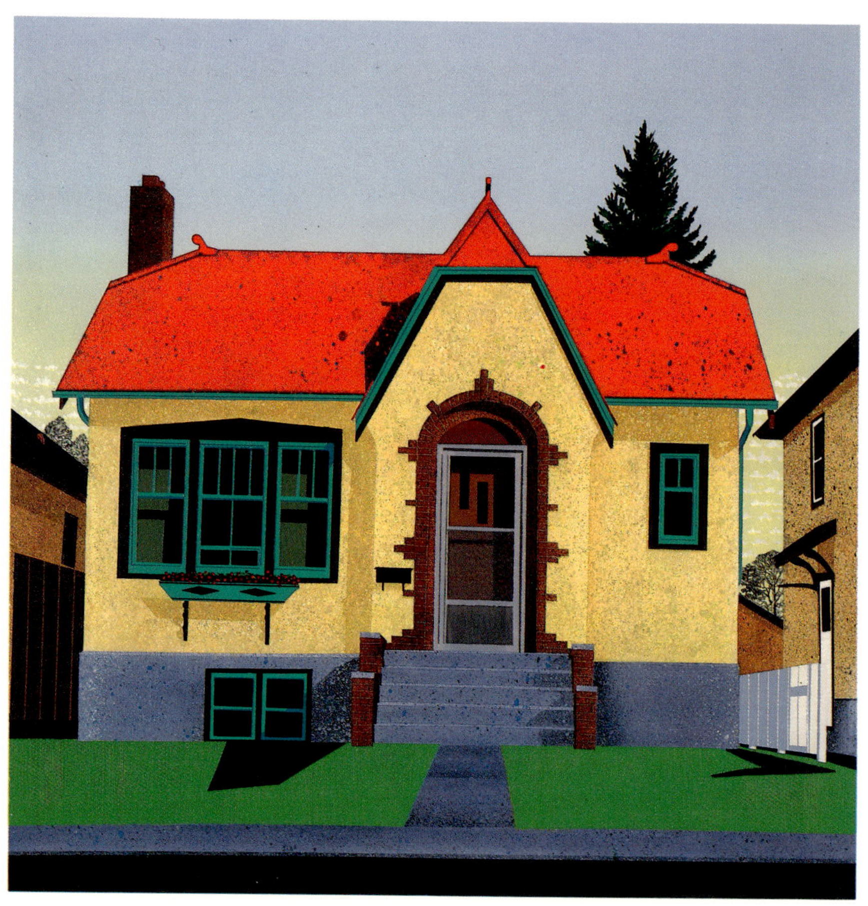

Plate 31 *Starter* 1986 (cat. 34)

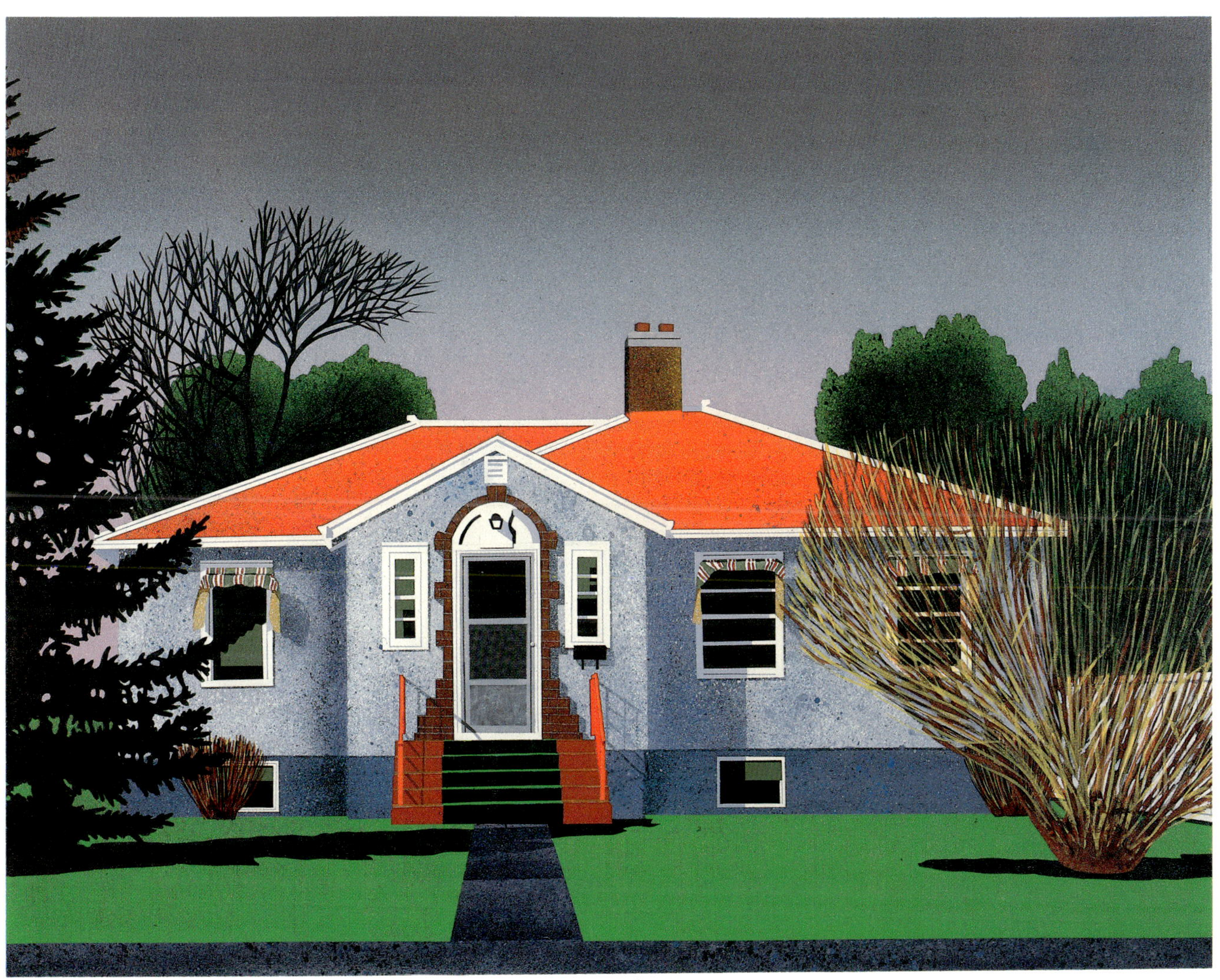

Plate 32 *Late Bloomer* 1986 (cat. 31)

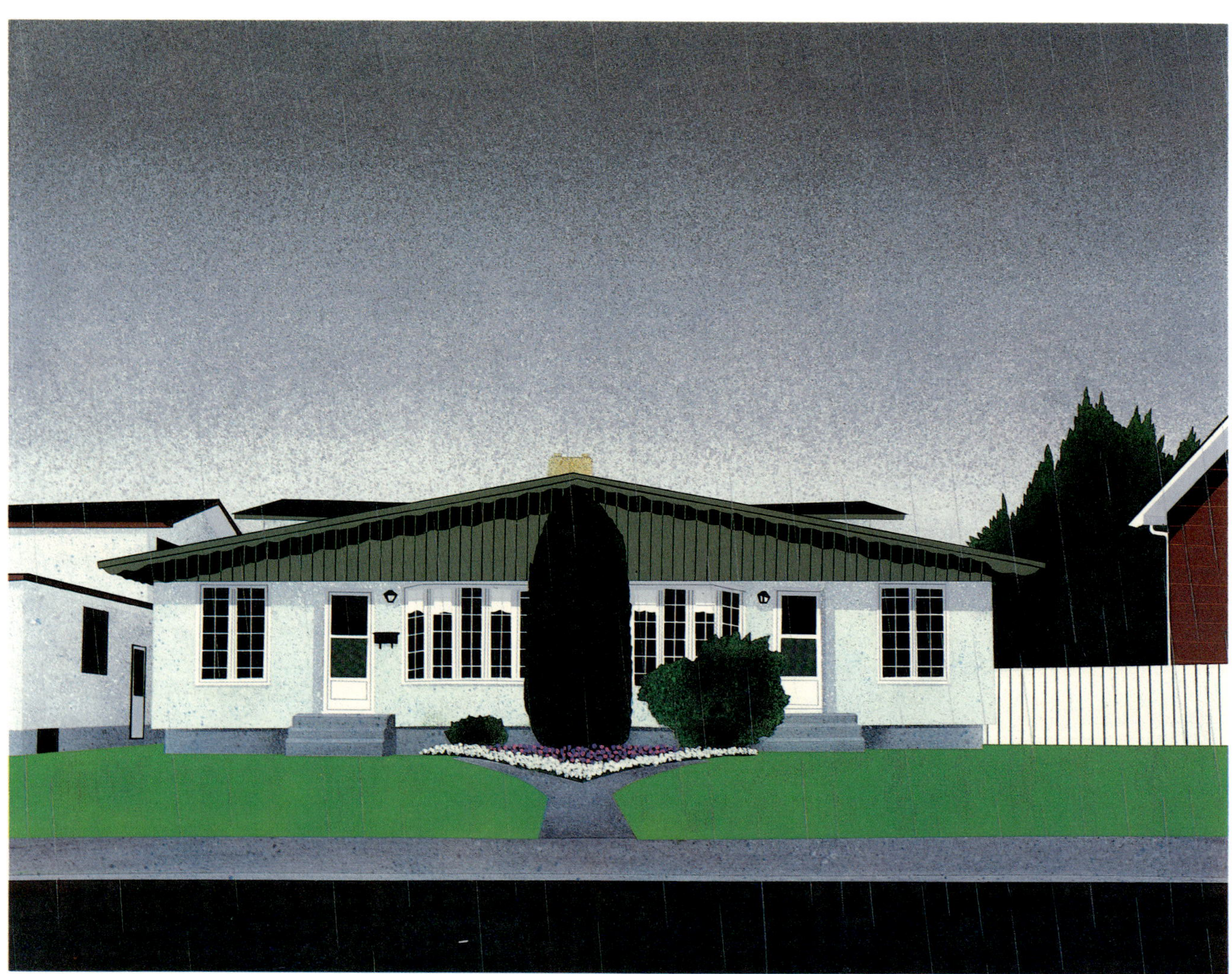

Plate 33 *Double Happiness* 1987 (cat. 36)

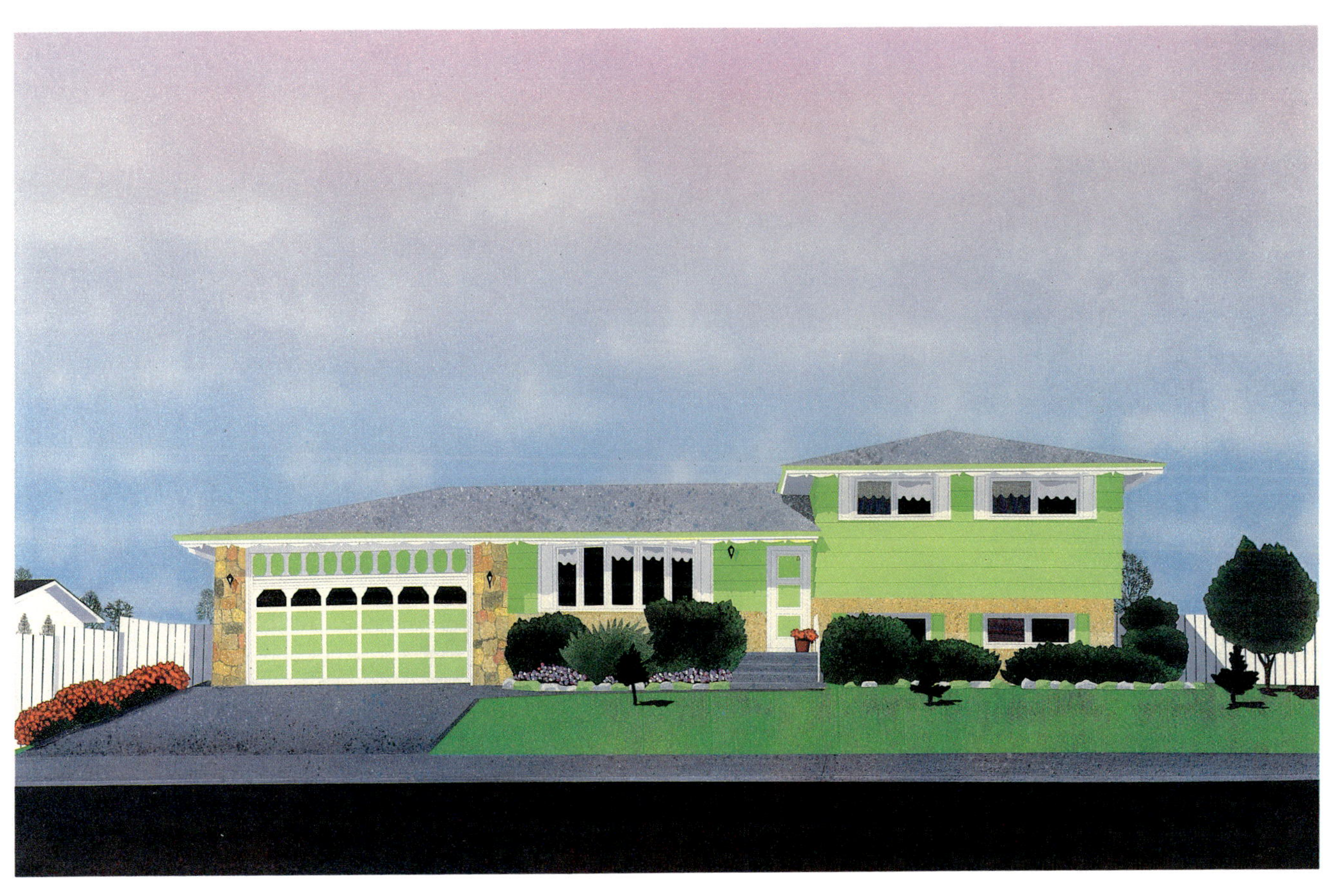

Plate 34 *Pride of Ownership* 1987 (cat. 38)

3. Eli Mandel, "Strange Loops," in Mandel, *The Family,* p. 19; originally published in *The Canadian Journal of Political and Social Theory,* Winter/Spring 1981.

4. See Eli Mandel, "Images of Prairie Man," in *A Region of the Mind: Interpreting the Western Canadian Plains,* edited by Richard Allen (Regina: Canadian Plains Study Centre, 1973), p. 206.

5. In his analysis, Mandel cites Northrup Frye's discussion of these questions in Frye's preface to *The Bush Garden* (Toronto: Anansi, 1971), pp. i-xi. See Mandel, "Strange Loops," pp. 19–20.

6. *"Grandfather's Painting:* David Thauberger," in Eli Mandel, *Life Sentence: Poems and Journals 1976–1980* (Victoria: Press Porcépic Ltd., 1981), pp. 27–28.

7. See Robert Stacey, " 'Bursting Through': The Poster Posterity of Andrew King," in *The Big Show! Andrew King's Show Prints, 1919–1958* (Regina: Dunlop Art Gallery, 1987), p. 25. For a history and analysis of oversized roadside statuary from an American perspective, see Karal Ann Marling, *The Colossus of Roads: Myth and Symbol Along the American Highway* (Minneapolis: University of Minnesota Press, 1984).

8. See David Thauberger's artist's statement in Karen Finlay, *D. Thauberger: Prints* (Toronto: Art Gallery of Ontario, 1984).

9. A comprehensive history and assessment of this important period in Saskatchewan has yet to be written. For general background see Christopher Varley, *Winnipeg West* (Edmonton: The Edmonton Art Gallery, 1982) and John King, "A Documented Study of the Artists' Workshop at Emma Lake, Saskatchewan, from 1955 to 1970," University of Manitoba, 1971. For a consideration of Greenberg's influence through an examination of his impact on one artist of the period see Helen Marzolf, *Kenneth Lochhead: Abstract Paintings 1962–1967* (Regina: Dunlop Art Gallery, 1988).

10. Donald Kuspit, "The Unhappy Consciousness of Modernism," in *The Critic is Artist: The Intentionality of Art* (Ann Arbor: UMI Research Press, 1984), p. 233.

11. Greenberg had a particularly healthy contempt for those he saw as "provincial." See, for example, his comments about Wassily Kandinsky and Marsden Hartley in Clement Greenberg, *The Collected Essays and Criticism,* vol. 2, *Arrogant Purpose 1945–1949,* edited by John O'Brien (Chicago and London: The University of Chicago Press, 1986), p. 3. Greenberg's hostility to differing positions is considered in Kay Larson, "The Dictatorship of Clement Greenberg," *Artforum* 25 (Summer 1987), pp. 75–78.

12. The 'hysterics' of California and Chicago art are seen by Donald Kuspit as a means of keeping "instinct" alive in art in the face of threats of assimilation by unified, cosmopolitan-based artistic theory and practice. See "Regionalism Reconsidered," in Kuspit, *The Critic is Artist,* pp. 283–90.

13. Portions of this part of this essay and the discussion of Thauberger's landscapes in the following section have appeared previously in somewhat different form. See Peter White, *Culture's Nature: Landscape in the Art of Gerald Ferguson, Jeffrey Spalding, Douglas Kirton and David Thauberger* (Regina: Dunlop Art Gallery, 1986) and *David Thauberger: Landscape Paintings* (Swift Current, Saskatchewan: Swift Current National Exhibition Centre, 1987).

14. The actual structure represented in *Crystal Palace* is the Great Palm House at Kew.

15. For a discussion of memory and history in postmodern culture, see William Olander, ''Fragments,'' in *The Art of Memory/The Loss of History* (New York: The New Museum, 1985), pp. 7–12.

16. E. L. Doctorow, *World's Fair* (New York: Random House, 1985), p. 265.

17. Ibid., p. 266.

18. Quoted in Helen A. Harrison, ''The Fair Perceived: Color and Light as Elements in Design and Planning,'' in *Dawn of a New Day: The New York World's Fair, 1939/40* (New York: The Queens Museum and New York University Press, 1980), p. 46.

19. Francis V. O'Connor, ''The Usable Future: The Role of Fantasy in the Promotion of a Consumer Society for Art,'' in ibid., p. 62.

20. Marshall Berman, *All That is Solid Melts into Air: The Experience of Modernity* (Harmondsworth: Penguin Books, 1988), p. 238.

21. For a discussion of the fair's architecture in the context of ''moderne versus modern,'' see Eugene A. Santomasso, ''The Design of Reason: Architecture and Planning at the 1939/40 New York World's Fair,'' in *Dawn of a New Day,* pp. 39–40.

22. The building represented in *All That Glitter,* the Regina head office of the Saskatchewan Power Corporation, was designed by Joseph Pettick. Pettick also designed the Regina city hall. Though this building is less successful, its presence, combining the modernist high-rise with Venetian motifs, has nonetheless made it a distinctive civic symbol. Thauberger has also painted this building (*City Hall Painting,* 1981; The Saskatchewan Arts Board Permanent Collection).

23. For a recent history of the suburb, see Robert Fishman, *Bourgeois Utopias: The Rise and Fall of Suburbia* (New York: Basic Books, 1987).

24. Quoted in Kate Flint, ''Fictional Suburbia,'' in *Popular Fictions: Essays in Literature and History,* edited by Peter Humm, Paul Stigant and Peter Widdowson (London: Methuen, 1986), p. 124.

25. Ibid.

26. Witold Rybczynski, *Home: A Short History of an Idea* (New York: Penguin Books, 1987), p. 13.

27. Eli Mandel, ''Academic and Popular,'' in *The Family,* p. 57.

BEYOND CONTEXT:
DAVID THAUBERGER'S ART COLLECTION

For almost as long as he has made art, David Thauberger has also collected it. His collection is large, impressive and includes a high percentage of works that are of unusual quality or interest. Thauberger's Saskatchewan folk art collection is of major importance while the works of major contemporary artists he has acquired — primarily prints — are inevitably strong or revealing examples of the work of those artists. Like his art-making, Thauberger has approached collecting in a highly directed, purposeful way. Though it is by no means inclusive, an inventory of his collection breaks down into several distinct groups; in addition to Saskatchewan folk art, these include other folk, outsider and popular art; Regina and prairie contemporary art; Chicago, California and western American art and international Pop and other graphic art.

From a consideration of the content of Thauberger's collection, a useful index of the range and nature of his artistic interests emerges. ''Having it all around has created a certain context within which my own work functions or operates for me.'' However, while the collecting practices of artists inevitably involve context, they often express concerns and values that go beyond it. In Thauberger's case, this is apparent in the comprehensiveness and very particular structure of his collection and, crucially, in the passion with which it has been and continues to be assembled.

Thauberger first became interested in the idea of collecting through the California artist David Gilhooly, an avid collector himself who taught at the University of Saskatchewan in Regina from 1969 to 1971. Thauberger did not begin to collect seriously, however, until he returned to Regina several years later from graduate school in the United States. The impetus was provided by his discovery of folk art in Saskatchewan. In a relatively brief time Thauberger made contact with many of these artists, developing close friendships with a number of them. In these interactions there was a kind of reciprocal process. For most of the artists it was the first time anyone had taken a serious interest in what they were doing or responded to them as a peer. For Thauberger, the situation was a revelation. ''Here was a whole community of artists living around me, concerned with all of my own art concerns. Their influence on me was immediate and profound.''

In folk art, Thauberger found an example of how, in contrast to artworld orthodoxy, a serious art practice not only could be carried on in a place like Saskatchewan but could be based on it. This was perhaps the major factor for Thauberger in establishing a perspective and point of view as an artist himself. The key was that making art and his own deeply felt attachment to the province and his rural roots need not be incompatible. Beyond the rich formal possibilities it suggested, for Thauberger having this work both cemented emotional and personal bonds with these artists and represented his own acceptance of where he lived. In addition, in response to what for the most part at the time was a lack of interest in folk art on the part of Saskatchewan's public art institutions, Thauberger acquired this work with a mind to its preservation. He subsequently became involved in a number of Saskatchewan folk art exhibition and publication projects. Beyond the impact of such efforts in promoting awareness and appreciation of folk art, these activities integrated with Thauberger's own work in terms of a broadened sense of artistic purpose and responsibility, in this case not only to a particular group of artists but to a place.

It has been suggested that art that involves a regional perspective not only reflects that particular culture but in fact contributes to defining it. If Thauberger's own art from this period began to do just this, his involvement with folk art also participated in that process. In each case, concepts of

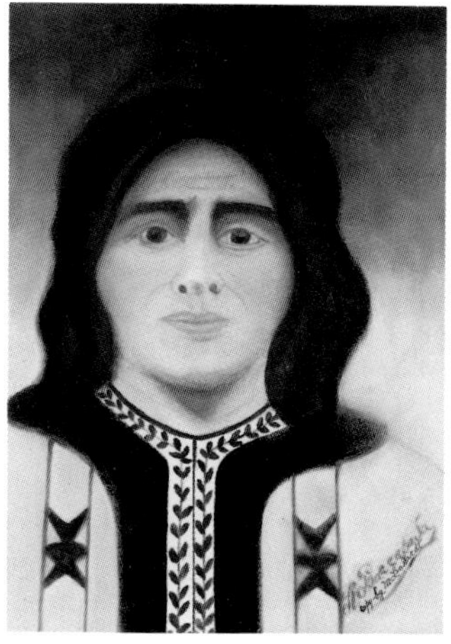

Molly Lenhardt
Untitled ca. 1972
Oil on canvas board
45.6 × 35.5 cm

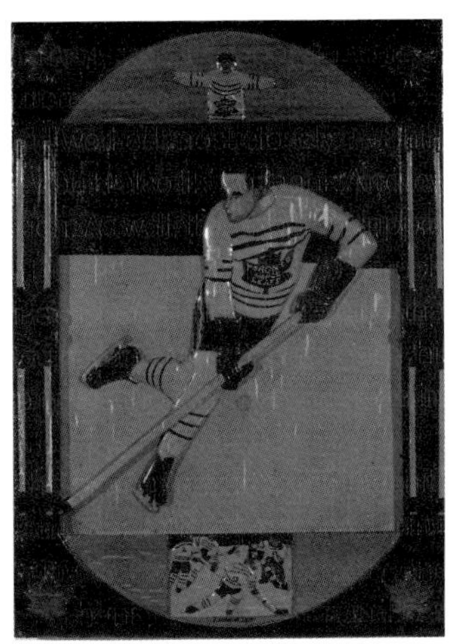

Sam Spencer
Charlie Conacher 1930
Wood, enamel and laquer on
carved wood
49.0 × 35.6 cm

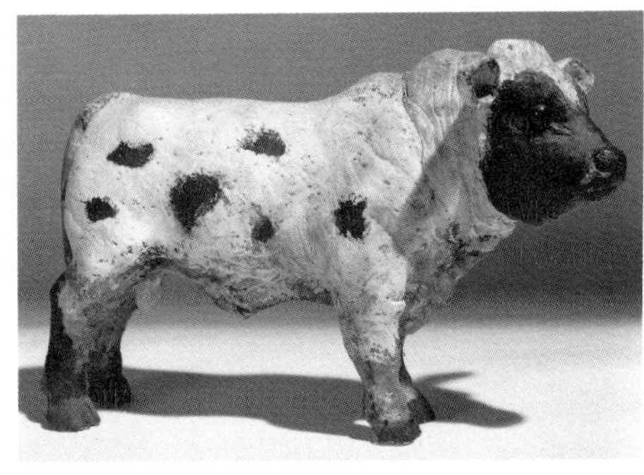

Joe Fafard
Rogers Bull 1973
Clay and acrylic paint
21.5 × 35.0 × 14.2 cm

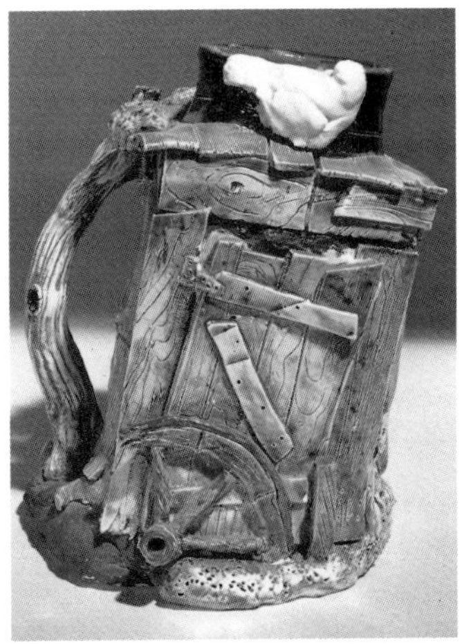

Victor Cicansky
Outhouse Cup 1972
Clay and glaze
22.4 × 19.5 × 13.6 cm

Roy De Forest
Untitled 1971
Pastel, charcoal and felt marker on paper
56.5 × 76.5 cm

Joseph Yoakum
*Little Colorado River Through Navaho Indian
Resivation Near Cameron, Arizona* 1970
Pastel, ballpoint pen, felt-tip pen
and colour pencil
30.7 × 48.0 cm

Scottie Wilson
Untitled n.d.
Enamel on commercial ceramic plate
30.5 × 26.4 cm

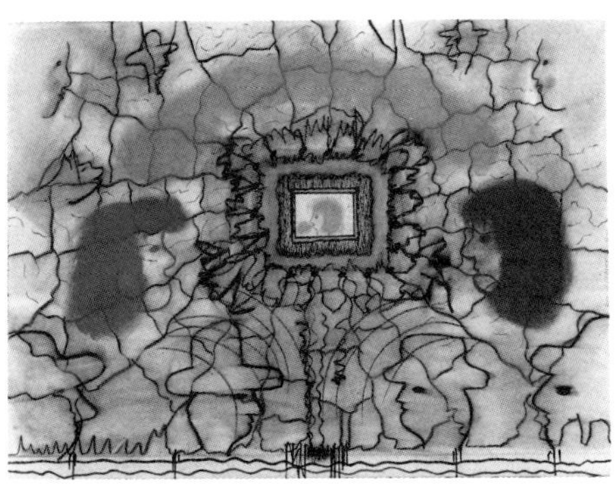

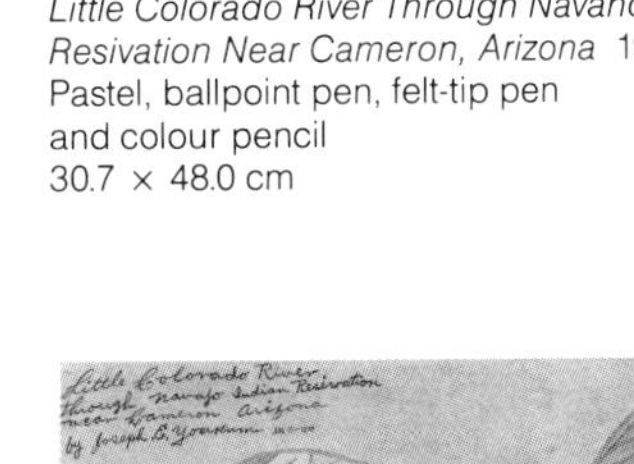
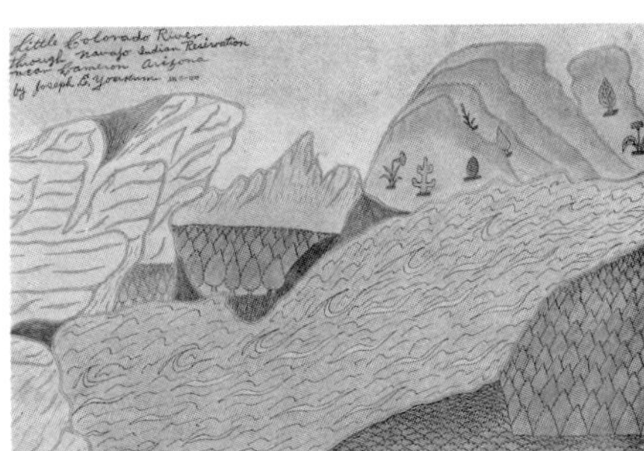

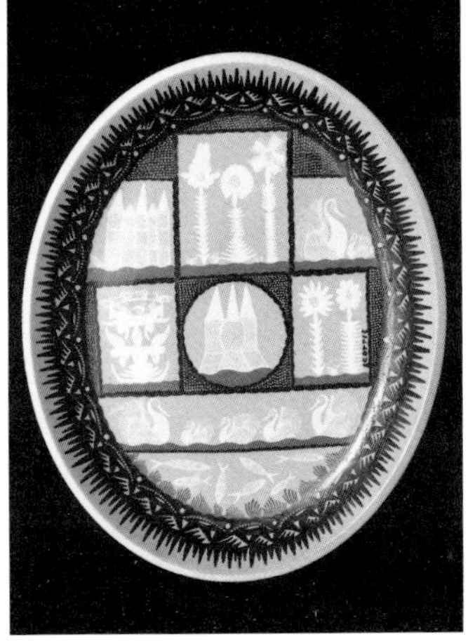

community and identity are critical. For Thauberger this has inevitably involved the works of artists with whom he has felt a sense of solidarity based on similar attitudes about region and place. In this regard, Thauberger has been associated most notably with Regina artists Joe Fafard and Victor Cicansky. Yet it is perhaps as interesting that he has expressed or defined this idea of community through the consistent acquisition of works by younger local and other prairie artists with whom he feels common ground is shared.

To this more specific sense of community can be added an extended community of artists, only a few of whom, such as Gilhooly, he has known but whose work has had an affect on him. What is perhaps interesting here is the extent to which these works and artists *live* for Thauberger. In a 1985 artist's statement, Thauberger dealt very little with his own work. Instead, he concentrated on his formative experiences as an artist. The following concerns the year (1971–72) he spent in Sacramento at California State University:

> ...it was there that art, especially contemporary art, unfolded for me. There were more artists living and working there than I had imagined. The energy around the place was incredible. Artists on faculty included Joseph Raffael, Jim Nutt, Steve Kaltenbach, Karl Wirsum, and Gladys Nilsson.
>
> This was the first time I had seen so much contemporary art and the experience changed my life. All the artists were teaching, but were mainly making fantastic art. I recall weekly lectures that included presentations by artists then working in the Bay area. Many exhibitions stood out, but some, such as Roger Brown's show at Sacramento State, Claes Oldenburg's *Object Into Monument* and William Wiley's *Wizdumb,* both at Berkeley, are particularly memorable to me.
>
> At this time I began to paint as a direct result of seeing Wiley's retrospective . . . and several Wayne Thiebaud paintings . . . At this time I really began to pay attention to Pop art (especially Lichtenstein and Dine), Chicago Imagist painting (Nutt, Brown, Paschke and others) and California painting (especially Wiley, Thiebaud, Raffael and De Forest).

Here is a whole nexus of interrelated influences, interests, attitudes and values encompassing, among other things, a preference for graphic and iconic figuration, formal expression that is emphatic, an emotional realm arising from an appreciation of naive and popular art and artifacts and, in many cases, a strong feeling for place. However, as it was with respect to the folk artists in Saskatchewan, what is perhaps most revealing in the context of this discussion is Thauberger's relationship to these artists. If he has assiduously collected almost all of them over the years, it unquestionably relates to the way in which they are experienced as part of his own experience. Reference points as well as cues for memory, these works narrate and constantly feed back not simply on his art but on his history and career as an artist.

Functioning very much emotionally and psychologically, collecting connects Thauberger to individuals, experiences and art that have both been important to him and have affirmed him in his activity as an artist. In this sense, collecting is not simply an adjunct to making art but is integral to what he understands his practice as an artist to be. Moreover, given the ardent and, indeed, autobiographical nature of his collection, an inevitable conclusion is that through collecting Thauberger articulates and reinforces for himself a strongly held conviction about the actual importance, richness and value of art.

P. W.

A Partial List of Artists Represented in David Thauberger's Collection

Saskatchewan Folk Art
Eva Dennis, Wesley Dennis, Ed Fletcher, Ann Harbuz, Laura Harness, Molly Lenhardt, Roland Keevil, W. C. McCargar, Harvey McInnis, Fred Moulding, Sam Spencer, Dmytro Stryjek, Jeanne Thomarat, Robert Vincent

Other Folk, Outsider and Popular Art
Levine Flexhaugh, Jahan Maka, Joe Sleep, Scottie Wilson, Joseph Yoakum, unknown Mexican and European artists and artisans

Regina and Prairie Contemporary Art
Gisele Amantea, Lorne Beug, Ron Bloore, Bob Boyer, Cyndy Chwelos, Victor Cicansky, Jerry Didur, Joe Fafard, Chris Finn, Brian Gladwell, Richard Gorenko, Bill Lobchuk, Billy J. McCarroll, Don Proch, Jack Severson, Tony Tascona, Russ Yuristy

Chicago, California and Western American Contemporary Art
Rudy Autio, Clayton Bailey, Roger Brown, Roy De Forest, Robert Else, David Gilhooly, Luis Jimenez, Steve Kaltenbach, Gladys Nilsson, Ed Paschke, Maija Peeples, Joseph Raffael, Wayne Thiebaud, William T. Wiley

International Pop and Other Graphic Art
Patrick Caulfield, Louisa Chase, Jim Dine, Julia Healy, David Hockney, Allen Jones, R. B. Kitaj, Roy Lichtenstein, Mimmo Paladino, Frank Stella, Andy Warhol

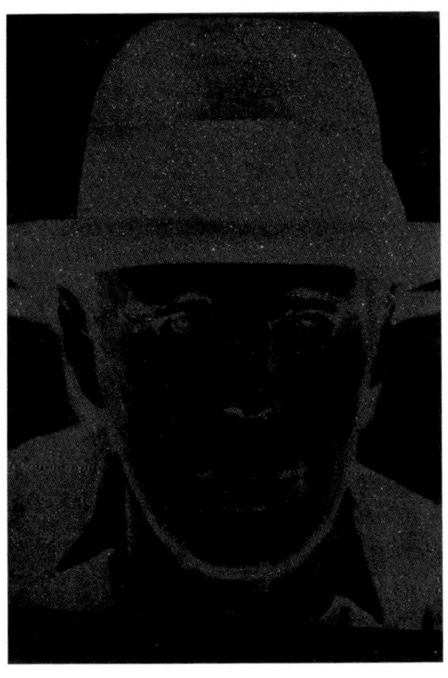

Andy Warhol
Joseph Beuys — Red and Black 1980
Screenprint with diamond dust
111.7 × 83.9 cm

Roy Lichenstein
Mirror #7 1972
Lithograph and screenprint
96.3 × 62.4 cm

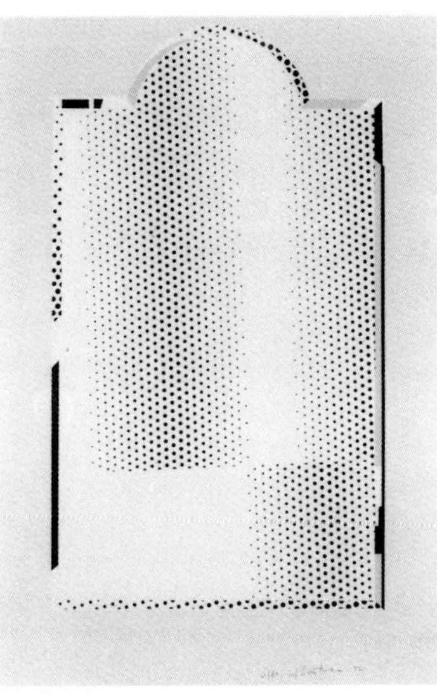

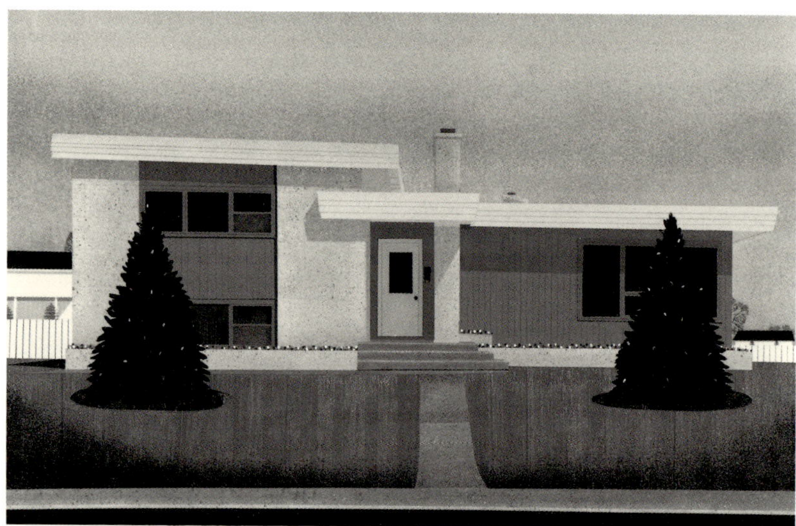

Fig. 14 *50s Split* 1987 (cat. 37)

1. *Grandfather's Painting* 1978
Acrylic and glitter on canvas
140.3 × 156.8 cm
Ann and Eli Mandel, Toronto

2. *Green and White Painting* 1978
Acrylic and glitter on canvas
114.3 × 175.9 cm
University of Lethbridge;
Gift 1985 of Mr. Jeffrey Spalding

3. *Crystal Palace* 1979
Acrylic and glitter on canvas
121.9 × 198.1 cm
Private Collection

4. *Harvest Painting* 1979
Acrylic and glitter on canvas
167.6 × 228.6 cm
Susan Whitney and Stephen Arsenych, Regina
(Exhibited in Regina only)

5. *Night Lilies* 1979
Acrylic on canvas
173.9 × 243.8 cm
Patricia and Clifford Wiens, Regina

6. *Rainbow Danceland* 1979
Acrylic and glitter on canvas
131.2 × 181.0 cm
Glenbow Museum, Calgary;
Purchase 1980 with funds
provided by The Canada Council
and Esso Resources Limited

7. *Slough* 1979
Acrylic and glitter on canvas
173.9 × 243.8 cm
Private Collection

8. *All That Glitter* 1980
Acrylic and glitter on canvas
167.6 × 228.6 cm
Dr. and Mrs. James McNally, Providence Bay,
Ontario

9. *Bread and Butter* 1980
Acrylic and glitter on canvas
114.3 × 172.7 cm
Potash Corporation of Saskatchewan,
Saskatoon

10. *Dance Hall* 1980
Acrylic and glitter on canvas
114.9 × 172.7 cm
Mendel Art Gallery, Saskatoon
(Exhibited in Regina and Saskatoon only)

11. *Dream Home (Ethnic Version)* 1980
Acrylic and glitter on canvas
114.9 × 172.7 cm
Norman Mackenzie Art Gallery, Regina;
Gift 1981 of Mr. Douglas Rawlinson

12. *Green and White Painting
(Dobberville)* 1980
Acrylic on canvas
167.6 × 228.6 cm
The Canada Council Art Bank

13. *Grey Painting* 1980
Acrylic and glitter on canvas
114.3 × 175.9 cm
Private Collection

14. *Kachina* 1981
Acrylic and glitter on canvas
114.9 × 172.7 cm
Toronto-Dominion Bank

15. *Light Shower* 1981
Acrylic and glitter on canvas
167.6 × 229.2 cm
Bank of Montreal
(Exhibited in Regina only)

16. *White Hall* 1981
Acrylic and glitter on canvas
229.2 × 167.6 cm
Art Gallery of Hamilton;
Gift 1982 of the Volunteer Committee

17. *Lake Reflecting Mountains* 1982
Acrylic on canvas
167.6 × 228.6 cm
Private Collection

18. *Seeing Double* 1982
Acrylic and glitter on canvas
114.3 × 172.7 cm
Husky Oil, Calgary

19. *the rocky mtns* 1982
Acrylic and glitter on panel
111.8 × 180.3 cm
The Canada Council Art Bank

20. *Big Geyser* 1983
Acrylic and glitter on canvas
203.2 × 127.0 cm
The Saskatchewan Arts Board Permanent
Collection

21. *Honeymoon Nights* 1983
Acrylic and glitter on canvas
111.8 × 172.7 cm
Gordon Capital Corporation, Toronto
(Exhibited in Regina only)

22. *Observation Point* 1983
Acrylic, glitter and letraset on canvas
172.7 × 111.8 cm
Macdonald Stewart Art Centre, Guelph;
Purchase 1983 with assistance
from The Canada Council

23. *Driving Rain* 1984
Acrylic, glitter and nails on canvas
111.8 × 172.7 cm
Jay Scott

24. *Machu Picchu* 1984
Acrylic and glitter on canvas
228.6 × 167.6 cm
Courtesy of the Artist

25. *Black Rain* 1985
Acrylic, glitter and drill bits on canvas
111.8 × 172.7 cm
The Saskatchewan Arts Board
Permanent Collection
(Exhibited in Regina only)

26. *Intermittent Shower* 1985
Acrylic, glitter, letraset and
sewing needles on canvas
111.8 × 172.7 cm
Gerald W. Schwartz, Toronto

27. *Little Dream Home* 1985
Acrylic, glitter and letraset on canvas
55.9 × 55.9 cm
Victor S. Ford, Toronto

28. *Motel — 24 Channels* 1985
Acrylic and letraset on canvas
33.0 × 71.8 cm
Private Collection

29. *Some Acid Rain* 1985
Acrylic, glitter, letraset and nails on canvas
167.6 × 228.6 cm
Stephen Arsenych and Susan Whitney,
Regina

30. *Corona North* 1986
Acrylic and glitter on canvas
111.8 × 172.7 cm
Rodger Linka, Regina
(Exhibited in Regina only)

31. *Late Bloomer* 1986
Acrylic and glitter on canvas
111.8 × 137.2 cm
Canada Mortgage and Housing Corporation

32. *Parachute Jump* 1986
Acrylic, glitter and colour pencil on canvas
177.8 × 116.8 cm
The Canada Council Art Bank

33. *Space Bridge* 1986
Acrylic and glitter on canvas
116.8 × 177.8 cm
University of Lethbridge;
Purchase 1986 with funds provided by
the Alberta Advanced Education Endowment
and Incentive Fund

34. *Starter* 1986
Acrylic, glitter and screen on canvas
111.8 × 111.8 cm
McMillan, Binch, Toronto

35. *Steel Pavilion* 1986
Acrylic, glitter and letraset on canvas
116.8 × 176.5 cm
Art Gallery of Windsor

36. *Double Happiness* 1987
Acrylic, glitter and screen on canvas
109.2 ×142.2 cm
Courtesy of Susan Whitney Gallery, Regina

37. *50s Split* 1987
Acrylic, glitter and letraset on canvas
111.8 × 172.7 cm
Courtesy of Susan Whitney Gallery, Regina
(Exhibited in Regina only)

38. *Pride of Ownership* 1987
Acrylic, glitter and letraset on canvas
109.2 ×172.8 cm
Courtesy of the Artist

39. *Doll's House* 1988
Acrylic, glitter and letraset on canvas
142.2 × 142.2 cm
Mr. and Mrs. Franklin Silverstone, Montreal

BIOGRAPHY/BIBLIOGRAPHY

David Thauberger was born in 1948 in Holdfast, Saskatchewan. He was educated at the University of Saskatchewan, Regina (B.F.A. 1971), California State University, Sacramento, California (M.A. 1972) and the University of Montana, Missoula (M.F.A. 1973). He organized *Grassroots Saskatchewan,* the first major exhibition of Saskatchewan folk art, for the Norman Mackenzie Art Gallery, Regina, in 1976 and the exhibition *Harvey A. McInnis* for the Mendel Art Gallery, Saskatoon, Saskatchewan, in 1981. He has worked for the Saskatchewan Arts Board as Visual Arts Assistant (1974–1978) and Visual Arts Consultant (1983–1985). His paintings are included in major public and private collections in Canada and he has been the recipient of numerous awards and commissions. Since 1973 he has lived in Regina.

Selected Solo Exhibitions

1971
David Thauberger, Memorial University Art Gallery, St. John's, Newfoundland (travelled)

1972
Jennifer Pauls Gallery, Sacramento

1973
Dunlop Art Gallery, Regina

1975
Rosemont Art Gallery, Regina

1977
Shoestring Gallery, Saskatoon

1978
Kesik Gallery, Regina

1979
David Thauberger — Prairie Pictures, Dunlop Art Gallery (travelled)

1980
David Thauberger, Glenbow Museum, Calgary, Alberta

1981
Susan Whitney Gallery, Regina

David Thauberger: Paintings, 49th Parallel Centre for Contemporary Canadian Art, New York, New York

1982
Galerie Don Stewart, Montreal, Quebec

Gallery Don Stewart, Toronto, Ontario

Mira Godard Gallery, Calgary

David Thauberger (national travelling exhibition organized by Dunlop Art Gallery; calendar)

1983
Gems of the Yellowstone, Susan Whitney Gallery

Mira Godard Gallery, Toronto

1984
David Thauberger: Works on Paper, Susan Whitney Gallery

D. Thauberger: Prints, Art Gallery of Ontario, Toronto (brochure; essay by Karen Finlay; travelled)

1985
David Thauberger, Canada House Cultural Centre, London, England (brochure; essay by David Burnett)

Mira Godard Gallery, Toronto

Susan Whitney Gallery

1986
Woltjen/Udell Gallery, Edmonton

1987
Mira Godard Gallery, Toronto

Susan Whitney Gallery

David Thauberger: Landscape Paintings, National Exhibition Centre, Swift Current, Saskatchewan (brochure; essay by Peter White)

Selected Group Exhibitions

1970
Funk 3, Burnaby Art Gallery, Burnaby, British Columbia

1971
Northern California Arts, Jennifer Pauls Gallery

1973
Ceramics International, Alberta College of Art Gallery, Calgary (catalogue)

1974
New Clay in Regina, Norman Mackenzie Art Gallery

Nine Out of Ten, Art Gallery of Hamilton, Hamilton, Ontario (catalogue; travelled)

Western Canadian Painting: The Prairies, Saidye Bronfman Centre, Montreal

1976
Joe Fafard/David Thauberger, National Exhibition Centre, Swift Current

Messages from Southern Saskatchewan, Dalhousie University Art Gallery, Halifax, Nova Scotia (catalogue)

Seven Ceramic Sculptors, Southern Alberta Art Gallery, Lethbridge (brochure)

1980
Artists as Printmakers, The Art Gallery at Harbourfront, Toronto

The Continental Clay Connection,
Norman Mackenzie Art Gallery
(catalogue; essay by Maija Bismanis)

Pluralities 1980, National Gallery of
Canada, Ottawa, Ontario (catalogue;
essay by Philip Fry)

1982
The Saskatchewan Open, Mendel Art
Gallery

1983
New Perceptions: Landscapes,
The Art Gallery at Harbourfront
(catalogue)

*The Grand Western Canadian
Screenshop: A Print Legend,*
Ukrainian Cultural Centre,
Winnipeg, Manitoba (catalogue)

1984
Regina Collects, Norman Mackenzie
Art Gallery (catalogue)

1985
*The Second Generation: Fourteen
Saskatchewan Painters,* Norman
Mackenzie Art Gallery (catalogue;
essay by Michael Parke-Taylor and
Norman Zepp)

1986
*Culture's Nature: Landscape in the
Art of Gerald Ferguson, Douglas
Kirton, Jeffrey Spalding and David
Thauberger,* Dunlop Art Gallery
(catalogue; essay by Peter White)

Double Takes (travelling exhibition
organized by Saskatchewan Writers
Guild; brochure)

Saskatchewan: A Sense of Place,
Rosemont Art Gallery (catalogue)

1987
True North/Far West, Rosemont Art
Gallery and University of the Pacific
Gallery, Stockton, California
(catalogue; essay by Clyde
McConnell)

Selected Bibliography

Adamson, Arthur. "The Grand
Western Canadian Screenshop
Retrospective." *Arts Manitoba,* vol. 3,
no. 2 (Spring 1984): 17–18.

Burnett, David and Schiff, Marilyn.
Contemporary Canadian Art.
Edmonton: Hurtig Publishers, 1983:
282–83.

Borsa, Joan. "The Second
Generation: Fourteen Saskatchewan
Painters." *Vanguard,* vol. 14, no. 10
(December 1985/January 1986): 40.

Enright, Robert. "The Second
Generation: Fourteen Saskatchewan
Painters." *Canadian Art,* vol. 2, no. 4
(Winter 1985): 84.

Ferguson, Bruce. "Made in
Saskatchewan." *Canadian Antiques,*
vol. 2, no. 12 (October 1980): 11–12.

Handforth, Robert. "Pluralities 1980."
Artscanada, no. 238–39
(December 1980/January 1981):
35–39.

Keziere, Russell. "Ambivalence,
Ambition and Administration."
Vanguard, vol. 9, no. 7 (September
1980): 8–13.

Mandel, Eli. "A Comprehensible
World: The Work of Cicansky,
Thauberger, Yuristy and Fafard."
Artscanada, no. 230–31
(October/November 1979): 15–19.

Mays, John Bentley. "Will the Real Mr.
Thauberger Please Stand Up." *The
Globe and Mail,* August 9, 1980: 11.

——————. "A Hard-Eyed Look
Beyond Landscape." *The Globe and
Mail,* November 19, 1983: 13.

Monk, Philip. "A Clearing House of
Trends." *Maclean's,* July 28, 1980:
50–51.

Murray, Joan. "David Thauberger:
Popular Imagery King." *Vie Des Arts,*
vol. 31, no. 124 (September 1986):
44–47.

Tousley, Nancy. "Thauberger Lauds
Folk Artists." *The Calgary Herald,*
October 8, 1980: B13.

——————. "David Thauberger:
Paintings, Drawings and Prints."
Parachute, no. 22 (Spring 1981):
47–48.

——————. "Thauberger Takes a
Postcard Holiday." *The Calgary
Herald,* August 19, 1982: C6.

——————. "Culture's Nature:
Landscape in the Work of Gerald
Ferguson, Douglas Kirton, Jeffrey
Spalding and David Thauberger."
Canadian Art, vol. 4, no. 2
(Summer 1987): 100–02.

——————. "Prairie Vernacular."
Canadian Art, vol. 4, no. 3.
(Fall 1987): 86–93.

Visions: Contemporary Art in Canada.
ed. Robert Bringhurst, Geoffrey
James, Russell Keziere and Doris
Shadbolt. Vancouver/Toronto:
Douglas & McIntyre, 1983: 58.

Webb, Marshall. "Read: Landscape."
C Magazine, no. 9 (Spring 1986):
75–76.

ACKNOWLEDGMENTS

Throughout the organization of this exhibition I have benefited from the advice, cooperation and support of many people. Coordination of exhibition details with the Mackenzie Art Gallery went smoothly from the start. I would like to express my particular appreciation to those at the gallery with whom I worked most closely — Shirley Bracewell, Andrew Oko, Bonnie Schaffer and Betty Stothers. I would also like to thank Andrew Oko for providing me with the opportunity to organize this exhibition. As well, the ongoing support of the staff of the Dunlop Art Gallery and Ron Yeo, Chief Librarian, Regina Public Library, is much appreciated.

For their assistance in locating works, thanks are extended to Susan Whitney of the Susan Whitney Gallery, Regina, and Mira Godard and Philip Ottenbrite of the Mira Godard Gallery, Toronto. I would also like to thank those individuals and institutions who provided me with access to works in the course of research.

One of the many pleasures of the exhibition has been working with Nancy Tousley. Her written contribution is only one aspect of what in many ways has been a collaborative approach in identifying and developing the ideas and concerns expressed in this publication.

Finally, my thanks go to Ronnie and David Thauberger, good friends with whom I have enjoyed many experiences, not the least of which has been working on this exhibition.

Peter White